# *Did You Ever Meet Hitler, Miss?*

## A Holocaust Survivor Talks to Young People

'ALL HUMAN BEINGS ARE BORN FREE –
AND IN EQUAL RIGHTS AND DIGNITY'
Article 1, Universal Declaration of Human Rights

I would like to dedicate this book to the memory of my husband Franz Levi. He always supported me in my work and was my sternest critic – always constructive. I miss him very much.

# The Beth Shalom

# Holocaust Centre

Britain's first Holocaust memorial and education centre, Beth Shalom, opened in 1995. It was the private initiative of two brothers, Drs Stephen and James Smith, who were not motivated by any personal or family connection with the events of the Holocaust, as they had none. They believed that the destruction of European Jewry should matter to everyone. They felt that Britons should remember it and learn from it, and face the challenge it poses to the values we hold and the kind of society we choose to create.

Since 1995, the Centre has gained a national and international reputation for the sensitivity and professionalism of its work. It houses a permanent exhibition on the Holocaust, a library and seminar facilities, and is set in landscaped memorial gardens. It is visited each week by hundreds of students taking part in school visits, and by members of the general public. As well as spending time in the museum and gardens, all of the young people who visit with their schools also have an opportunity to meet and hear a survivor of the Holocaust.

Survivors form a vitally important part of the life of the Centre, and make an irreplaceable contribution through their first-hand accounts of those tragic events and their willingness to share their painful memories with today's young people. Soon their lessons will be legacies, and the generations that follow will have to carry the message they are trying to convey.

In the conversations between survivors and students many questions and answers emerge which may not at first be apparent. In dialogue and discussion, these perspectives develop into an important and revealing conversation. This book has come into being in recognition of the importance of those conversations. The legacy that survivors leave is more than a narrative of what happened to them; it is also the complex of questions their stories raise.

# Did You Ever Meet Hitler, Miss?

## A HOLOCAUST SURVIVOR
## TALKS TO YOUNG PEOPLE

Dr TRUDE LEVI

Beth Shalom
Holocaust Centre

in association with

VALLENTINE MITCHELL
LONDON • PORTLAND, OR

First published in 2003 in Great Britain by
VALLENTINE MITCHELL
Crown House, 47 Chase Side
London N14 5BP

and in the United States of America by
VALLENTINE MITCHELL
c/o ISBS, 5824 N.E. Hassalo Street
Portland, Oregon, 97213-3644

Website: www.vmbooks.com

British Library Cataloguing in Publication Data

ISBN 0-85303-467-2 (paper)

Library of Congress Cataloging-in-Publication Data

A catalog record for this book is available
from the Library of Congress

Typeset in 10/13pt Palatino by Vallentine Mitchell
Printed in Great Britain by MPG Books Ltd, Bodmin, Cornwall

# Contents

# List of Illustrations

# Acknowledgements

I was very pleased when the idea came up for a book with the students' questions and my answers. However, I was fully occupied with a heavy schedule of lectures both in this country and in Germany. Having suggested that the students could send me questions which I would answer, I needed someone to help me with the preparation of the material. First, the material had to be copied, as I did not want to lose the originals. My wonderful friend Renie Inow undertook the donkey work and copied the letters at the Holocaust Survivors' Centre in London. I am deeply obliged to them and thank them most sincerely. I also had an offer of help from Eva Davis, who had some time on her hands. She sorted out all the letters with questions in them and also examined the questions to avoid any duplication. I was very grateful for her assistance and would like to thank her. Eva then started working again and I needed an editor. On the train to a lecture at Trinity Hall, Cambridge, at the invitation of the Students' Union, a young man approached me. He told me he had heard me speaking; he had also read my book, *A Cat Called Adolf*, and seen me participating in a debate on a TV programme. He himself had just won the award of Young Reporter of the Year and was finishing his degree at Cambridge. This young man was Johann Hari and I would like to thank him warmly for introducing me to Anna Powell-Smith. As we conversed, I mentioned the idea of the Questions and Answers book and said that I was looking for an editor. He replied that he was sure he could find me one. By the time I returned home that evening and opened my e-mail, I had an offer from a young woman, namely Anna. She was finishing her degree and had some previous experience in editing, she wrote. She would be pleased to help me. And so we got together and started several months of very fruitful and friendly co-operation. I am much in debt to Anna for all the wonderful effort she put into the realisation of the project. She had a really tough time transcribing the two interviews recorded at Beth Shalom Holocaust Memorial Centre in Laxton, Nottinghamshire.

The project was proceeding but no deadline had yet been fixed. At the end of November 2001, I came back exhausted from a punishing schedule of talks in Germany. A German friend was coming to stay with me for a long weekend. Then suddenly a message came from Anna: the manuscript had to be completed, possibly the week before Christmas. It was too late to cancel my friend's visit. I apologised when I told her that I would have to do some work during her stay. As she is a retired English teacher who now devotes most of her time to Holocaust education in Frankfurt, she insisted on helping me. During the four and a half days she was with me, we spent our time mostly at the computer, working. On my own I would not have been able to cope in time. To Renate Rauch go my most deeply felt thanks. Luckily, she found the project interesting and worth the time spent on it.

Another great friend, Trisha Ward, though not physically involved in the book, was always in the background with advice, encouragement and warnings when it came to diplomatically touchy questions and problems. Before my husband's death, he used to fulfil this role when I wrote, and I would like to thank Trisha for all the support she has given me in the last few years.

Wendy Whitworth from Beth Shalom had the overall supervision of the editing of the book. We initially spent a day together going through all the material, correcting my grammatical mistakes, with which she gently confronted me – though it was no confrontation – luckily I know my limits and am always ready to accept criticism. I enjoyed every minute of the time spent with Wendy and owe her deep thanks. Since that first workday, we have spent many hours together, either meeting, or by e-mail or phone. I am convinced that without her help, I would not have been able to reach our aim of producing this book.

It was Dr Stephen Smith, one of the Directors of Beth Shalom Holocaust Centre, who had the idea for publishing this book. I met Stephen before he even opened the Holocaust Centre, and have been working in conjunction with the Centre for the past seven years since its foundation. I admire the work of the Smith family and am always happy to be associated with them. They are a most admirable, devoted and wonderful team, sparing no time or effort for their role in Holocaust Education. And so, I would like to thank Stephen and his staff for publishing this volume.

Frank Cass, Director of Vallentine Mitchell Publishers, produces a series of Holocaust memoirs, although my own book, *A Cat Called Adolf,* was less of a memoir of the actual events than a description of the consequences, both physical and psychological, of having endured two concentration camps and a death-march. According to my contract, I had to offer them first refusal on the publication of this book. We did this quite late in the process, but I did not anticipate any difficulties. I was amazed when Frank Cass told me that he was also interested in publishing it. Luckily, he and Stephen Smith came to an agreement to publish the book jointly. I thank Frank Cass for being so accommodating and for coming to a friendly, collaborative publishing arrangement with Stephen and his staff.

Many thanks to David Blunkett for his Foreword to this book. I very much appreciate his kind words and thank him for them. David Blunkett, currently Home Secretary, was approached for his comments on this work whilst he was still Secretary of State for Education. I hope that my own experiences as an asylum-seeker – though at the time not to this country, where I came in 1957 as a Commonwealth subject – will serve as a guide for continual sensitivity and fairness when the Home Office considers all asylum-seekers, now and in the future.

Rabbi Julia Neuberger also most generously agreed to write the Introduction to the book and I owe her a great debt and very sincere thanks.

And one more acknowledgement: this is to e-mail, because without it we could not have ping-ponged our problems back and forth without wasting time.

*Trude Levi*
*2002*

# Foreword

Trude Levi's work is a reminder of the human tragedy at the heart of the Holocaust. Her powerful writing highlights a personal dimension to this dark, terrible event in the history of humanity.

Reading about the past is vital to ensuring that our children grow up aware of the past, learning from history as they form the future.

The Holocaust must never be forgotten. In combating prejudice and racism, we need to remind people of how the lessons of history must be vigorously implanted in the minds of those whose vigilance will be needed to avoid such horrors occurring again. This is an important book which demands to be read.

*Rt. Hon. David Blunkett MP, Home Secretary*

# Introduction

Trude Levi tells her story with astonishing simplicity. There is little elaboration of what happened to her – just the bare, horrible, facts. And the fact that her story is so spare in the telling gives it all the more impact: the reader has to ask himself or herself whether they would have behaved in the same way if they had been there, whether they would have been as brave, as dignified, as tough, as determined to survive without losing their principles.

Most of this volume is an anthology of questions asked in letters to Trude Levi, and her replies. Does she hate the Germans? This wise woman objects to any group being classified like that. What Germans? All Germans? But there were German people who behaved magnificently and German people who stood out against the horrors and German people who lacked courage but nevertheless showed occasional kindness. Trude Levi hates people being lumped together – and others saying: 'I hate Jews, or Germans, or foreigners, or gypsies.' For there is good and bad in everyone, although she does tell the story of how she had been taught that people who appreciate music could not be all bad, and there was a guard in the camp who loved music, and asked a prisoner who was a musician to play for him, but was nevertheless a sadist and a horrible man.

But why is this volume important? It is important not only because of Trude Levi's own story, her own loss of family, her own fractured relationship with some of the family that survived, such as her brother. Her own story is important, of course. But she uses it to tell a wider tale, to illustrate, in unsentimental, accurate, cool detail what it was like to be sent to Auschwitz, or to other camps. She was a victim of the Nazi outrage against the Jews. She was classed as vermin by them, and treated like vermin. Yet she survived to tell the tale, of her own experience, and of others who did not live to tell their own stories.

Trude Levi has given the latter part of her life to this 'new' life's work. She wants us all to know what it was like, to understand what it meant to lose everything as a very young woman, to menstruate for the last time for years, to starve, to walk barefoot over stones, to go on forced marches, to collapse, and by luck, not to be shot. She wants us to know because such cruelties are not over. The Holocaust was uniquely planned, uniquely huge, uniquely horrible. But such destructions of populations have not ceased. The technologies are improving – it is even more possible now to kill millions than it was between 1939 and 1945. Trude Levi wants us to understand what happened and its uniqueness. But she also wants to show us that aspects of what happened are repeatable, are easy, are attractive to the weak and the pathetic, the prejudiced and the cruel. And she wants us to understand that categorising any group into subhuman can lead to this destruction, this *Shoah*, this appalling decimation of human life.

But, alongside all this, she wants us to understand the very practical. She did survive. The Frenchman who promised to help her and marry her turned out to be a complete charlatan, a thief and a dishonest man. He took advantage of her at her weakest, just as hope was dawning. But, even then, she survived. She did eventually get British citizenship, she did become a librarian, and even now, in her late 70s, she is able to carry on with her career of teaching us about what happened. And the very practical, the detail, is enough to enlighten us about what the life must have been like for the camp inmates – but also to make it clear that some aspects of her life, particularly just after the war, are similar to what current asylum-seekers go through. She is sympathetic to asylum-seekers, and critical of governments who try to keep them out and make their lives a misery. She was, of course, an asylum-seeker herself.

My mother, who came to Britain in 1937 as a domestic servant, from Germany, was also an asylum-seeker. So were my uncle, my grandparents and many other relatives. We know the heart of the asylum-seekers – and we also know that few people choose to leave their homes and family unless things are truly terrible where they come from. Of course there are economic migrants – but they are different. Throwing up your chances and leaving, just like that, is difficult and hugely threatening. And tough, and terrifying, and often quite confusing and unwelcoming when you arrive at one of your possible destinations.

All this is part of Trude Levi's story. And all this has much to teach us. Young people – children and students – asked her question after question. She never balks at giving her answers. Her answers tell you about how she views fairness, about how she views hardship, about how she thinks that those who perpetrated evil deserve punishment, about how she cannot forgive the perpetrators – only those who are dead as a result of their actions could do that. And she also tells us about how she thinks we should behave to each other – not a religious woman, she thinks that we should never do to others what we would not wish them to do to us. Do only to others what you wish them to do to you. A golden rule – and emotionally tough in the wake of her experiences. But, more than anything, her answers tell us about Trude Levi, survivor *par excellence*, and someone who has a story to tell that will make us all think, and reconsider how we treat anyone different from ourselves. And how we group people together, categorise them, and somehow think people of one group or another are all the same. Trude Levi makes it clear that they are not, and that each human being has to be viewed as an individual, with an individual conscience, and individual set of beliefs, and their own way of behaving. Even the mostly bad can sometimes be good. And even the very good can sometimes be terrible. There is no absolute – except in the knowledge of the evil human beings can inflict on one another, and that human watchfulness should be able to prevent it, but often does not.

*Rabbi Julia Neuberger*
*2002*

CHAPTER 1

# Why I Choose to Tell My Story*

When I first started to speak publicly about my experiences in the Holocaust, way back in the 1980s, I had no idea that my talks would provoke literally hundreds of letters and e-mails, containing thousands of questions, from schoolchildren and students in England and Germany. But I felt instinctively that every letter and every question was important, and answered every single one personally. Wherever I went to speak, I always ended my talk by saying that the students could write or e-mail any additional questions to my home address. Sometimes we simply did not have time for a question-and-answer session at the end. Sometimes the students seemed so stunned by what they had just heard that I knew there were latent questions which they could not express at that point. I felt they should be able to.

I have always replied to every question that is sent to me, however silly it may seem, including 'Did you ever meet Hitler?' and 'What would you say to Hitler if you saw him?' I have even sometimes replied when there were no questions, but the letter raised important issues. So I would make up my own question and write back anyway! That's another reason it seems important to me to write back in reply; I do not like to leave students in a vacuum.

---

* Adapted from an interview with Trude Levi conducted by Stephen Smith at the Beth Shalom Holocaust Memorial Centre, 20 September 2001.

And that, in a nutshell, is how this book of letters came into existence, although back in the 1980s the idea had not yet germinated. It was only many years later, after a great deal of experience of talking to young people about the Holocaust, that I understood the importance of those letters in terms of education, facing difficult issues and making real connections between people.

So, where did it all begin, and why? The first time I ever spoke publicly about my experiences during the Holocaust was in 1986, at a teachers' conference on racism, but I would have spoken out much earlier if the opportunity had ever arisen. Many years ago, I was a guide at an Anne Frank exhibition for schools and the organisers asked me to mention my time in Auschwitz. When I talked about the concentration camp, the children asked me a great many questions, and the teachers asked me to go and speak at their schools. I always agreed, but no invitation followed. So nothing ever came of it, and I was very sad about that at the time.

I first began to speak in 1989, to sixth-form and university students who were doing their research in the library where I worked and invited me to speak. Of course the real trigger for schools to come to my talks was *Schindler's List* in 1994. Though it's not the best film I have ever seen, and there are things in it I'm not very happy about, I still feel that it's the most important thing that happened to Holocaust education, because it touched people and made them think. The Holocaust became a real issue. From that moment on people started to take notice of survivors.

Later, the Holocaust Survivors' Centre in London started a public speaking course. That's when I really started speaking regularly, because they organised schools for us to visit. There were very few survivors talking of their experiences in those days, and so I did quite a lot of work with the Centre because I felt it was so important. Then, at an international teachers' conference where I spoke, I met Stephen Smith, who told me about his plans to set up the Beth Shalom Holocaust Centre in Laxton, Nottinghamshire. He asked me whether I would be interested in participating in his project as a guest speaker. And that's how I became more involved in speaking to teachers, students and universities.

If anyone had told me a few years ago that today I would be describing my experiences in front of audiences of hundreds of people, I would simply have laughed, because I used to be an incredibly shy person. My long-standing friends still don't understand how today I can speak so freely. Previously, when I was with friends, I would speak to one person, but if there were three of us, I hardly said a word. It must be because speaking publicly about my experiences in the Holocaust made me more confident. I saw that it worked. People understood, and the letters of thanks I received afterwards encouraged me. Then I started offering to answer questions at the end of the talk. If there was no time for a question-and-answer session, I would invite people to write to me. That's how I came to receive all these letters with questions, personal stories, photographs, even poems. They were important to me and I kept them carefully because they helped me to understand the educational impact a survivor could have on young people. And it was from that collection of letters that the idea for this book came to me.

\* \* \* \* \*

In England, I speak mainly to schools and universities, to groups of all ages from 13 upwards. Occasionally I speak to adults, at historical or charitable societies, teachers' conferences, and lately also on panels on Holocaust education. In general I prefer to speak to smaller groups, but sometimes I visit sixth-form conferences of about 120 students, where I give my talk first and then do workshops with smaller groups.

My talk generally lasts one and a quarter hours. I only omit things if I am not given enough time, but it is very difficult to choose what to leave out. If time is really short, I don't talk about the members of my mother's family who emigrated and managed to escape to other countries. The only allowance I make for younger audiences is that in a mixed group, I won't mention menstruation. It was truly horrible as we had no underwear, no access to water and no way to clean ourselves. Thirteen-year-old boys are too young not to be embarrassed, and giggling about such things is not appropriate.

If there is enough time, I like to have a ten-minute break between the talk and the questions, because I find that the pupils ask many more questions if they have the chance to talk to each other for a few minutes. However, it's very rare to be able to do this in England because the timetable seems more rigid. In Germany I always have a break and sufficient time. If the students want the talk to go on for longer, they are allowed to make up the missed time later. The German educational system seems to be much more flexible in this respect.

Many headteachers tell me that they have never seen the children sit so quietly as when I am talking. Well, it is a fascinating story I suppose, and full of drama. The children often say, 'We have read books and seen videos about the Holocaust, but it was never as real as when a survivor told us his or her story.'

That is why I go on speaking. I find that when I am describing my personal experiences, something seems to click. Once, at King's College,

London, I was invited to speak to the History Society, along with a survivor of the *Kindertransports*. The student organising the talk told me there might be only 12 people there, but when we arrived, there were 150 people in the room. After we had finished speaking, there were so many questions that the meeting continued for another hour and a half, until we received a message that the hall was needed for another meeting. Suddenly, as I was putting my notes together, four Arab students came up to me. There had been some troubles in Israel that week – we had nearly cancelled our talk for this reason – and I was a bit apprehensive as to what they might want. But the students just said, 'Thank you so much, it was the first time we ever really understood what happened in the Holocaust.'

* * * * *

From the start, I knew exactly the messages I wanted to get across in my talk. Firstly, I wanted to say that it is wrong to make generalisations about people, either about what happened then or about the world now. It is one of my strongest beliefs that we should never speak about people as 'the Jews', 'the Gypsies', 'the Irish', 'the English', but think of them as individual people, even if they form part of a group. Even in the worst times in Germany, there were Germans who were extremely courageous and risked their lives to hide people from the Nazis.

I wanted to illustrate this by mentioning that in the slave-labour camp where I worked, there was a German worker who was decent, who brought me bread and encouraging and hopeful news, and tried to help us as best he could. I wanted to tell people about the German guard who once spoke civilly to me when we found ourselves alone on a train. Amidst all the dehumanisation of the camp, there was a human voice there. Conversely, there were Jewish women who collaborated in order to save their own lives and in so doing, put the rest of us in danger. I wanted to show that in every group there are people with principles who will stand up to protect others. Even if it is a matter of life and death, not everybody will do anything to survive, no matter what the consequences for others. Choices can be made.

This was the second message I wanted to get across: that there were moral and personal choices. I wanted to show that we could and did put up resistance, even if it wasn't resistance in terms of attacking people, because it would have been suicidal to fight against soldiers with machine-guns. There were other kinds of resistance: for instance, in my slave-labour camp, there were a thousand Hungarian Jewish women. I was part of a small number who set up a sabotage group. Or another example: I decided not to

4

co-operate with the camp guards or the SS women guards. I pretended not to speak German, although it was really my mother-tongue.

And, finally, when I spoke, I wanted to tell people the truth. I wanted most of all to bring out in detail the proven facts, everything I could remember.

* * * * *

There are two questions which schoolchildren and students ask most frequently. The first is, 'What do you think of the Germans nowadays?', and the second, 'What did the Holocaust do to your religious beliefs?' When I am asked about the Germans, I say straight away that there is a problem with the question. We cannot talk about 'the Germans', because not all Germans acted in the same way. Even if we consider them as a whole, there are three generations living in Germany today. The first generation, my generation, includes many perpetrators. There were also some who were courageous, who tried to help, or did help; and bystanders who, though they did not agree with what was happening, did nothing to prevent it out of fear. The second generation is not guilty; they were children or not even born at the time; and the third generation, the schoolchildren of today, certainly cannot be blamed for what happened 60 years ago. The two later generations must not be made to feel responsible for what happened. Blame only creates hatred. But they need to understand what happened and come to terms with it. While I have not forgiven the people who murdered my family and friends, I certainly don't hate all Germans. I also make the point that Jews were killed in many other countries – Poland, Austria, the Ukraine, Hungary – so it's not as simple as just blaming Germany. Nothing is just black and white!

The other question which students often ask is, 'What could have been done to prevent the Holocaust?' This is a question about bystanders and responsibility, and my answer is always that I cannot judge those who stood by and let it happen, because I don't know what I would have done under those circumstances. Terrible things still happen in the world today, and though I am horrified and might make a donation to a relief effort, I don't go to the country myself to prevent them, nor do I attend demonstrations as crowds frighten me. However, on occasion I do speak out or write to protest or support an issue of moral importance.

I make it clear that most people *did* know that the camps existed, and they knew what their purpose was. Many of the first generation say, 'We knew nothing.' I do not accept this and try to explain why it cannot be true and that most people knew what went on. We slave-labourers were not invisible; we worked in factories side-by-side with Germans. We walked bare-foot and in rags through German villages; and if the locals had the opportunity, they would ask where we came from. All over Germany there were hundreds of factories where slave-labourers worked. The train drivers who took us to the concentration camps, the guards inside the camps, our own guards and many others, all had families and went home on leave, and they were not all silent about what they had seen.

A few years after the war, when I lived in South Africa, I met quite a number of Germans who always asked me what part of Germany I was from. When I told them I was not German and had never lived there, they would ask how I came to speak such good German. I would tell them about my mother having been Austrian, and then say, 'I was in Germany during the war because I was deported there.' And if they replied, 'Oh, we didn't know anything about what was happening to the Jews,' then I was usually rather rude to them. It simply isn't true that people didn't know. But if someone said, 'I was a teacher, I had three children to feed and I couldn't afford to lose my job, so I looked away,' I could excuse that. I know that I too sometimes look away and don't want to get involved.

The most important and interesting topics for me are questions on ethnic minorities, on race, hatred and generalisation. I think it is very important to teach children not to generalise. I always say that it's very difficult to prevent oneself from doing it, that I have difficulties too. Sometimes I catch myself making generalisations without thinking and it makes me very sad. I always try to correct myself, because it is really important to stop.

The one question that I dread having to answer in Germany is, 'I love my grandparents but they won't tell me what they did during the war. What can I do about it?' I have a great deal of difficulty answering this because I could never set a child against his or her grandparents. My reply depends on how I am feeling; I either say it's not a question I am able to answer, or something like, 'Maybe you should try asking them again, it's very important and very healthy for people to face up to their past. Perhaps you can make them talk. But it doesn't mean that you should love them less.'

Students in Germany seem much more mature and are very open in the questions they ask. I have been asked, for example, 'What did you do about sex, did you masturbate?' In an English school that question would never come up. German students, I am sorry to say, usually ask more intelligent questions, and their letters are of a higher quality, although this is more true of pupils in former West Germany than in the East.

* * * * *

What do I hope will come out of the work I do? Well, I know that for the pupils my talk isn't just another lesson: it goes on being discussed in school. I even get letters from students who did not attend my talk, but want to ask questions anyway. It seems to stick in people's minds, to make a real impression, which is the most important thing. Sometimes I have received second letters, three or four years after a student first wrote, saying, 'I'm now at university doing a course on the Holocaust as part of my studies. I kept your first letter, because I want to show it to my grandchildren, so that they too will understand what happened, and nobody will ever forget.' And that, in just a few words, is why I carry on.

CHAPTER 2

# Surviving Inevitable Death: A Personal Testimony*

I was born Gertrud Mosonyi in a small town in Hungary called Szombathely, on 23 April 1924. My father was a doctor, a gynaecologist and GP, and he was also very involved in left-wing politics. He gave lectures and wrote articles on socialism, but he mostly spent his time trying to help other people, particularly the poor. Today there is a plaque on the house where we lived commemorating him which reads: *Dr Dezsö Mosonyi, the doctor of the poor, was deported from this place on April 22nd 1944.* The Nazis deported him for being a political activist, along with other opponents of Hitler, before the rest of the Jews were deported from Szombathely.

In his spare time my father was an amateur violinist and viola player, and he was the first person to write about the psychology of music. He wrote a book on the subject in German, but as it was completed in 1934, it was not published in Germany because there were restrictions on the publication of books by Jews. However, he contributed an article on the subject in the same year to Freud's journal, *Imago*, and it is still quoted today. In any book on the psychology of music, my father's name appears in the index quite extensively. Altogether, he had a brilliant mind and was a highly respected man.

* Adapted from an interview with Trude Levi conducted by Stephen Smith at the Beth Shalom Memorial Centre.

My mother was a language teacher from Vienna and gave private lessons in our home. She was also very cultured and interested in everything around her. With my mother I always spoke German, but to my father and my friends I spoke Hungarian. I grew up bilingual, but by the age of 11 I actually spoke four languages. My mother taught me English, and one of my uncles by marriage, whom I was very fond of, was French. I always adored the language and used to listen to it on the radio as though it were music.

We were not especially well off, and it was always difficult paying the rent on our flat because most of my father's patients were poor and paid him in eggs, chickens or other home-grown products rather than in money. One of his female patients, who had a baby every year, was married to a cobbler who made new shoes for us every six months, and a furniture-maker who also had a large family made wonderful modern furniture for our home.

Nonetheless, we had a lively and interesting home, with lots of friends coming round for dinner parties. We played chamber music at home, and had many musical scores and some beautiful though not very valuable paintings. We had over 3,000 books which I catalogued when I was 14. It was my first experience of librarianship and I would later become a librarian.

I had a brother five and a half years older than me who was a very gifted young pianist. When he was 18 and had finished school, he was admitted to the Music Academy in Budapest. Unlike my brother, I wasn't a very good pupil at school. I could only learn from the teachers I liked. The subjects I did well in were French, German, Art and Music. I was also good at Mathematics, despite the fact that our Maths teacher was rather anti-Semitic. But in other subjects I did less well; in History I did extremely badly because my teacher was very anti-Semitic, and in Hebrew reading, I felt the teacher disliked me. I couldn't learn from people I disliked. Ironically, I became a Hebrew teacher later in life and worked in libraries which specialised in history.

I was taken out of school at the age of 15, not because I was a bad pupil, but because in 1938 Hitler annexed Austria. Members of my mother's family in Vienna who managed to escape advised that I should leave school and learn a trade, which would be more useful if we had to emigrate or were taken away to a camp. That is how I became a milliner's apprentice and spent two years learning how to make hats. In the meantime I continued to study privately with my father every day.

When I finished my apprenticeship – having hated every minute of it – I was sent to sewing school for a few weeks. I knew that I wouldn't be able to go to university or college because of the restrictions imposed on Jews by the Hungarian government, but I decided that I would really like to be a nursery school teacher. I had always worked with small children and taught German to children during my holidays.

Luckily for me, in 1941, the Jewish community in Budapest opened a training college for thirty girls each year. Though they usually only took people with the equivalent of A-levels, I passed a three-day entrance test and was admitted in 1942. I moved to Budapest, completed an intensive one-year course to become a nursery school teacher and at the end of it, the college sent me out on short-term jobs to see how I performed as a teacher. In January 1944, I was appointed assistant to the professor who ran the training college's model nursery. I was very proud of this achievement.

\* \* \* \* \*

By January 1944 it was quite obvious that Germany was going to lose the war, and we thought it would all be over very soon. Since the Hungarian Jews were the last left in Europe, we believed we were the lucky ones. We suffered rationing and other restrictions, and our men were away in the army, but we still lived a relatively normal life compared to Jews in all the other countries. Well, we were wrong. On 19 March 1944, the Nazis occupied Hungary and from then on things moved very fast indeed.

The first restriction they imposed on all Jews was wearing the yellow star. Before the Nazi occupation, the yellow star was nowhere to be seen in Hungary. Three days afterwards, all the shops were inundated with them: the whole thing was completely planned and prepared. On the very day the yellow star was introduced, I went into hospital with a perforated colon and had a very serious operation. Four days later, all the patients were thrown out of the Jewish hospital because the Germans took it over, so I was in a pretty bad condition physically.

Some courageous Christian friends had offered to hide me and keep me safe, but my parents wanted me to go home. I was most grateful to my friends, but chose to go home and stay with my parents, because the last time I had been at home, six weeks before the occupation, I had had a bad argument with my father and had gone back to Budapest without even saying goodbye. I wanted to make up with him.

By then, Jews were only allowed to travel with a special permit, so I had to wait for permission to go back to Szombathely. I applied on 23 or 24 March, a few days after the occupation, and the permit eventually arrived on 22 April, allowing me to travel on the 24th. I phoned my father and told him I would be home in two days' time. It was my 20th birthday on 23 April, and my father said we would celebrate a day later when I got back.

On the train, I had to wear a very large yellow armband as well as the yellow star. I had to show my permit, a big piece of yellow paper, to anyone who asked how a Jew had the audacity to be on the train. I was only permitted to sit down if there was an empty seat, as I was not allowed to sit next to another person, to speak to anyone or visit the restaurant car or lavatory. It was a very slow train, stopping everywhere, so it would take me eight hours to get home. In fact, the journey actually lasted longer than that because on the way there was an air raid. The train stopped and we had to get out and lie down on the embankment. Nothing happened, but it delayed us even further and this caused me great trouble when I arrived in Szombathely.

We did not arrive in my hometown until five minutes past six in the evening. The problem was that Jews were not permitted to be on the street after 6 pm, nor were they allowed to take the tram. I was carrying a rucksack, a suitcase and a cello, and had to walk through the streets because I had no choice. I made very slow progress because people constantly stopped me and asked how I dared to be there. I had to show my permit; I was kicked, spat at, called 'dirty Jew' and 'Jewish pig'. This was my homecoming to the town where I was born. It ensured that I was never homesick again!

My mother was 49 years old and had always been a very energetic woman, young for her age. When I arrived home, I found her a collapsed, confused old lady. The flat was in complete disarray, with all our books thrown on the floor. In my father's surgery, his medical books and instruments lay on the floor in a heap. My father was not there. I eventually managed to find out from my mother that two days earlier, after my telephone call, two Hungarian gendarmes and two German SS had come to our house. They had rifled through all the books looking for subversive literature, and then they took my father away as a political prisoner. My mother had been unable to find out where he was taken, or even whether he was still alive. We would have no more news of him for the next two and a half months.

The next few days passed quickly. We had to hand in our bicycles, then our jewellery, then our savings account books and finally nearly all our cash. We were only permitted to keep a few pennies. On 7 May 1944 we had to move into the ghetto, taking only one piece of luggage with us. The ghetto consisted of two streets, right in the centre of town, separated off by barbed wire. We shared a small room with four other people; there was only one bed, so we slept on the floor. We were actually well off in comparison to others, as in some rooms up to 16 people had to live together. Men under 18 or over 50 (the others were in the Hungarian Army's labour camps), women and children, strangers, all had to share. We stayed there for seven and a half weeks. There was not much food, but we managed somehow.

* * * * *

At the end of June, we were told to take our one piece of luggage and were marched to the outskirts of the town to our first concentration camp, situated in a disused machine factory. The buildings were filthy and very polluted with oil, and the ground all around was equally saturated with oil.

Before we were taken into the camp, everyone was searched. Some people had managed to hide a gold chain, coin or gemstone by sewing it into their clothing. If it was found on them, they were beaten up so viciously that they were thrown into the camp half dead, or dead already. Since Szombathely was the main town in the county, all the Jews from the area were taken to this camp and 4,280 people were interned there. My mother and I slept on the ground outside. As it was a very hot summer, it didn't matter that we were outside, but the earth was filthy.

Early in the morning, I heard loudspeakers calling for 50 volunteers to go to a neighbouring town, although no further explanation was given. My mother and I had no reason to go, but I decided we absolutely had to volunteer. In fact, it was as though I was possessed. My mother didn't want to go, but I literally dragged her to the assembly place. There were already 49 people waiting when we arrived, and I actually pushed one older woman out of the group so that my mother and I could get in together. I behaved abominably, completely out of character, because usually I was a polite and decent human being. I am still not proud of my behaviour towards that woman, even today.

We were put onto a train along with the rest of the volunteers and after an hour, arrived at our second concentration camp, again situated in a disused factory. This one had barracks which must previously have been warehouses. There, we were divided into groups and each group was taken into one of these barracks. Nobody asked our names, nobody knew who we were. Yet, by pure coincidence, the first person we saw in our barrack was my father, of whom we had heard nothing for the last two and a half months. We were as happy as one can be under the circumstances. My father was a completely different person. Usually he was rather distant and not very emotional – I was only allowed to kiss him on birthdays or when returning from a long absence from home – but now he completely broke down and asked forgiveness for the row we had had.

We stayed in that camp for two days, and then we were put into cattle-trucks. The guards told us that we were 'privileged': the trucks usually held 70 to 90 people. They told us that only intellectuals and their families would travel in our truck, doctors, lawyers, architects and so on, and as a 'special privilege', there would be 120 people in our truck.

When they locked us in, we decided to deal with the situation in a civilised manner. We built benches from our luggage and sat on them, squeezed in tightly, back to back, with our knees up and our arms pulled in, managing somehow. There were two buckets for our human needs. We had to overcome our inhibitions and use them in front of strangers – men, women and children. Two buckets were not sufficient for 120 people, and at every jolt of the train, the muck spilled over. There was nothing we could do about it, so we sat in the muck.

The only openings for ventilation were two small holes, about two bricks long and one brick high, covered over with barbed wire, and we got very little air. It was very hot in the wagon and we quickly became dehydrated. I don't remember whether I had water with me. I suppose we probably drank all our water on the first day, thinking that there would be stops to obtain more. I remember I had a loaf of bread with me which I had baked the day before; in those days I always baked my own bread.

On the second day, the train stopped in the early afternoon and the SS guards shouted we had to get ready to get out. We demolished our 'benches' and stood waiting with our luggage until it got dark. When darkness fell, the train started again with a terrible jolt. We all fell over each other, and there was chaos. From that moment on, people became hysterical.

We were very thirsty. Everyone knows what thirst feels like, but this was a different kind of thirst. Our lips hurt because they were chapped with dehydration. We were hungry, but could no longer eat. I had a piece of bread in my hand, but could not swallow because my throat was so dry. People lost control, screamed, went mad, had heart attacks and died. We travelled with the dead, the mad and the screaming for five days and five nights.

\* \* \* \* \*

On the morning of the sixth day in the cattle-truck, 7 July 1944, the train finally came to a halt. The guards opened the doors and shouted at us to get out and leave our luggage. They told us we would be able to fetch it later, but of course we never saw any of our belongings again. During the

13

journey, my mother had completely collapsed, physically and mentally.

Once we were off the train, men and women were separated. That was the last time I ever saw my father. Then I was taken away from my mother when she was dragged off in a different direction, along with the rest of the older women and younger women with children under 14. All I can hope is that she was too far gone by then to understand what was happening to her. In that direction, we saw chimneys spewing out smoke, yellowish-pinkish in colour, with a terrible stench. At the time we did not know what caused the smell, but we soon found out that it was from the crematoria and burning bodies. This stench and smoke remained with us the whole time we were in this camp, Auschwitz.

Though we saw the ramp leading up to the crematoria and chimneys, we did not know what purpose they served. After the war, I found out that the ramp was actually built specifically for the Hungarian deportation, but at the time it never occurred to me that a country fighting a losing war might consider it a priority to drag away the last group of Jews, instead of using their manpower and rolling-stock for military purposes.

The younger women were then herded into a very large hall, which was ice-cold even though it was a very hot summer. We had to strip naked, then SS men came and shaved off every hair on our body before disinfecting us all over with some red liquid. Then we were thrown just one piece of clothing to wear, whether it fitted or not. We had no underwear, no shoes, just this one garment which was in fact taken from previous prisoners who no longer needed it.

I think we were in a state of shock. We did not understand what was happening to us. Apart from anything else, after our heads were shaved we could not recognise each other for some time, which was very frightening. And of course being shaved by men on all parts of our body was extremely humiliating.

Next we were herded out in rows of five and marched into another part of the Auschwitz-II complex: Birkenau-B2, which consisted of very large barracks. It was still near enough to the main part of the camp for us to smell the stench and see the smoke day and night all the time we were there. Inside the barracks, there was nothing except greyish-yellowish powdery soil. There were no trees or grass anywhere. The whole complex was surrounded by electrified barbed wire, watchtowers and soldiers with machine-guns and vicious guard dogs.

By the second day there, we had all developed dysentery, and during the night people often had to get up to visit the latrines. There were 1,200 women in the barracks, so it was incredibly overcrowded and we had to sleep sitting up, all crushed together, in the pitch black. When anyone got up to go to the latrines, they had to climb over the sleeping bodies. However, when people woke up in the dark and suddenly felt someone climbing over them, they were frightened and cried out. As soon as someone screamed, the soldiers would start to shoot into the barracks.

The latrines were guarded by SS men who found it very entertaining not to allow us to finish our business. Since we had no underwear and no access to water, neither to wash nor drink, and no way of cleaning ourselves except with our own clothes, we quickly became filthy and stayed that way the rest of the time we were there. We stank and when we sat on the ground, the powdery soil stuck to us. It was absolutely disgusting and there was nothing we could do about it.

A few days later, on the second or third day in the camp, we all started to menstruate. It was the last time we menstruated – the body does not waste its energies unnecessarily – but as we had no way of protecting ourselves, we were really in a terrible state. For me, that was the most horrible, the most dehumanising thing that happened. It was even worse than the five days in the cattle-truck. Everything else was terrible, but this was the worst of all.

\* \* \* \* \*

We were only allowed to stay in the barracks for a very short time at night, and the guards chased us out early each morning for roll-call. We stood in front of the guard-barracks in rows of five, waiting for the SS women to come and count us. In the open air we started shivering straight away. Birkenau had a very odd climate; even though 1944 was an incredibly hot summer, at night the temperature dropped to practically zero. Our one piece of clothing barely protected us at all from the cold. When the SS women finally arrived – often after we had been waiting for two or three hours – they were very bad at counting. Sometimes they had to count us more than once because all the numbers in the entire camp had to tally. Before sunrise, when it started to get warmer, many women collapsed and were dragged away.

After the SS women left, we waited in front of the barracks until our coffee arrived. Birkenau coffee was a lukewarm, brownish liquid, nothing like real coffee. But it was liquid, and for us liquid meant survival in that heat. As we had no access at all to water, every drop of fluid was vital. The coffee was poured into a casserole dish or a medium-seized pot, and we waited in rows of five to drink it. The first person in the row drank and passed the vessel on until it came to the fifth. Now I mentioned before that I was quite a decent human being and it was not in my nature to push people around, so I usually ended up in the fourth or fifth row, near the end of the queue.

The Jews in the camps were people just like anyone else. Some were aggressive and some were meek; some were selfish and some were caring. In these circumstances, some people were so determined to survive that they did anything they could to stay alive; they didn't care at all about their principles or their fellow-prisoners. These were the people used as our *Kapos* or supervisors, who were given the privilege of distributing the food. They stood in the first and second rows, so they got the coffee first and gulped down as much as they could. There was never very much left by the time the container reached the fourth or fifth row, but we did get something, even if it was very little.

While we stood there, people collapsed from dysentery, hunger or thirst. There were no trees or shade anywhere, and we didn't even have our hair to protect us, so women also collapsed from sunstroke. If they collapsed, they were dragged away and we never saw them again.

After the coffee, we were allowed to disperse. There was nothing to do; we either stood or sat around on the crumbly earth. At midday we were reassembled for our so-called 'lunch', which consisted first of soup served from a large cauldron. The people who distributed it never stirred the soup, so that anything in it stayed on the bottom of the pot. If we were lucky, there was a cabbage leaf floating in it or maybe a tiny piece of potato or shred of meat. Usually, when you were in the fourth or fifth row, there was nothing left in it. However, it was still liquid and therefore very important, even though the soup had little taste.

After the soup there was bread. The long, square loaves were supposed to be divided into eight pieces, but the people who distributed them cut them into nine or ten pieces, because an extra slice of bread was money. With bread they could buy cigarettes, matches, scarves, underwear or food; or they could eat it as an extra ration. And so the rest of us got even less than we were entitled to. With the bread, we usually got a piece of sausage, or quite a large piece of cheese, which was very tasty and very filling. There was only one problem – it was extremely salty and made you even thirstier. But if you didn't eat it, you stayed hungry. I always ate my cheese and bread straight away so that nobody could take it from me. For the next 24 hours there was no more food.

We were only once taken out of Birkenau-B2 camp during our time there, when we were sent out for a bath and given clean clothing. I had forgotten the incident completely until someone asked me one day whether any of the guards had ever hit me. Then it came back to me; we were walking barefoot over extremely sharp stones on our way to the bath. One of the stones rolled over and I slipped and stepped out of the line. The next second, I was lying on the ground. One of the guards had hit me so hard on the nape of the neck that I had blacked out for a moment and lost my balance. I managed to get up and back into the line before they could hit me again. Because I was concentrating so hard on where to tread, I remember very little else about the incident, where we were going or what the surroundings were like. But I do remember that this was the only time we left the camp.

* * * * *

This was our existence for four weeks in Auschwitz-Birkenau. Suddenly, on 2 August 1944, we were roused even earlier than usual, right in the middle of the night, and taken to the camp assembly-place. All the women from the barracks were lined up there in rows of five and we were ordered to strip naked for a medical inspection. It was freezing cold and we were very weak by that time, so again many women collapsed and were dragged away. While we waited, the sun came up and burned us, with the result that people also collapsed from sunstroke.

Finally, when it was nearly dark and the sun was setting, the Camp Commandant Hoess arrived, accompanied by the principal camp doctor, Dr Mengele. We had to pass in front of them, showing the palms of our hands, and sometimes Mengele said 'Open your mug!' ['*Mach Dein Maul auf!*'] and looked into our mouths. I don't know why, but maybe it was to see if we had any gold teeth. Anyway, he then said 'right' or 'left'. Those who went to the right were never seen again; that was the end of them. I was lucky; he sent me to the left.

Those of us sent to the left were the younger women and those who could still stand on their legs. We were taken into a shower room. By that time, we knew about showers that produced gas instead of water. It might have been three minutes or thirty seconds, but we seemed to be waiting there for an eternity. We were lucky; it was water that came from the showers. And what ecstasy it was to have water on our filthy bodies, to be able to wash ourselves again! Water on our tongues, in our mouths, to be able to drink! Nobody stopped to wonder if the water was poisoned – it was liquid, and that was all that mattered. We drank deeply, trying to soften our cracked lips.

Suddenly the water stopped and, dripping all over, we were herded into that very same ice-cold hall. Once more the SS men came and shaved off any hair that had grown in the past four weeks. After this we were given a wonderful plateful of cabbage soup and a chunk of bread. Then we were put onto another cattle-truck, less crowded than before, and we even had a thin layer of straw to sit on.

\* \* \* \* \*

We travelled through the night and the next day, and arrived at a camp in the centre of a small and pretty town called Hessisch-Lichtenau, some 27 kilometres from Kassel in the mid-west of Germany. We had now been transferred from the control of Auschwitz to that of Buchenwald, but we were not taken to Buchenwald itself, but to one of its 136 outcamps, Hessisch-Lichtenau. This seemed to me a beautiful camp because it had grass and trees, and I think even flowers. There were wooden barracks divided into rooms, each with 16 two-tier bunks. We all received our own bunk, a very prickly straw sack, a rough blanket, a bowl and a spoon. It was not very comfortable, but for the first time I had my own bed and blanket, so in comparison to Auschwitz it was heaven, absolute heaven. This would be our home for the next eight and a half months.

We arrived on 3 August, and the very hot summer continued. Nevertheless, the central heating was switched on, which encouraged hundreds of bedbugs to crawl out of the straw sacks. I always seemed to be a magnet for any kind of biting insect: the bugs would congregate on me, and so the others could sleep more easily. I usually managed about three nights in a barrack before I was completely covered in the things. During the winter, of course, the central heating was switched off!

In the camp at Hessisch-Lichtenau, there was a bathroom with lots of washbasins, each with a bar of soap on which was printed *Aus Judenfett gemacht* [made of Jewish fat]. I have since discovered that it is impossible to make soap from human fat; this has been proved by experiments. But that's what was indented on the soap. When I am speaking anywhere, I always make sure to mention what was printed on the soap, and what I have since learnt, because it is very important to me not to be accused of making false claims or elaborating on the facts.

We were also given shoes – or rather, those with normal-sized feet got shoes. On the uppers, the words *Aus Judenhaut gemacht* [made from Jewish skin] were printed. This was again untrue, because it is impossible to make shoes from human skin. People like me with very large feet did not have shoes. Instead, we were occasionally given wooden clogs, but clogs are very painful on bare feet, and break easily when you walk on uneven stones, which we did every day. There were never any more in stock, so I went barefoot most of the time, which was not very pleasant walking through pine forests, or through snow and ice. How I never had frostbite, I still do not understand.

ng-Jüdin

Vor- und Zuname: Gertrud Mosonyi    Haft Nr. 20607

Beruf: Lehrerin    geboren am: 23.4.24    in: Szombathely

Anschrifts-Ort

Eingel. am: 19.9.44    K.L.Auschwitz    Entl. am

Uhr von    Uhr nach

Bei Einlieferung abgegeben:

| | | | Koffer | Aktentasche | Paket |
|---|---|---|---|---|---|
| Paar Schuhe, halb. | Schlüpfer, Makko | Mantel: Tuch | Paar Handschuhe: Stoff | | Blechensack |
| Paar Schuhe, hohe | Leibchen | " Leder | Handtasche | | Invalidenkarte Nr. |
| Paar Schuhe, Haus | Korsett | " Pelz | Geldbörse | | Invalidenquittung |
| Paar Schuhe, überzieh. | Strumpfhaltergürtel | Jacke: Tuch | Spiegel | | Arbeitsbuch |
| Paar Strümpfe, Wolle | Unterrock | " Leder | Messer | | Photos |
| Paar Strümpfe, Seide | Bluse | " Pelz | Kamm | | Schreibpapier |
| Paar Söckchen | Kleid, Rock | " gestrickt | Ring | | |
| Hemd | Schürze: Kittel | Hut | Uhr m. Kette | | |
| Hemdhose | Schürze: Träger | Mütze | Uhr m. Armband | | |
| Büstenhalter | Taschentuch | Schal | Halskett. | | |
| Schlüpfer, Seide | Pullover | Paar Handschuhe: Wolle | Armband | | |

FIGURE 1: Prisoner's Personal Card: Transfer from Auschwitz Concentration Camp, Gertrud Mosonyi, Hungarian Jewess. Prisoner Number 20607.

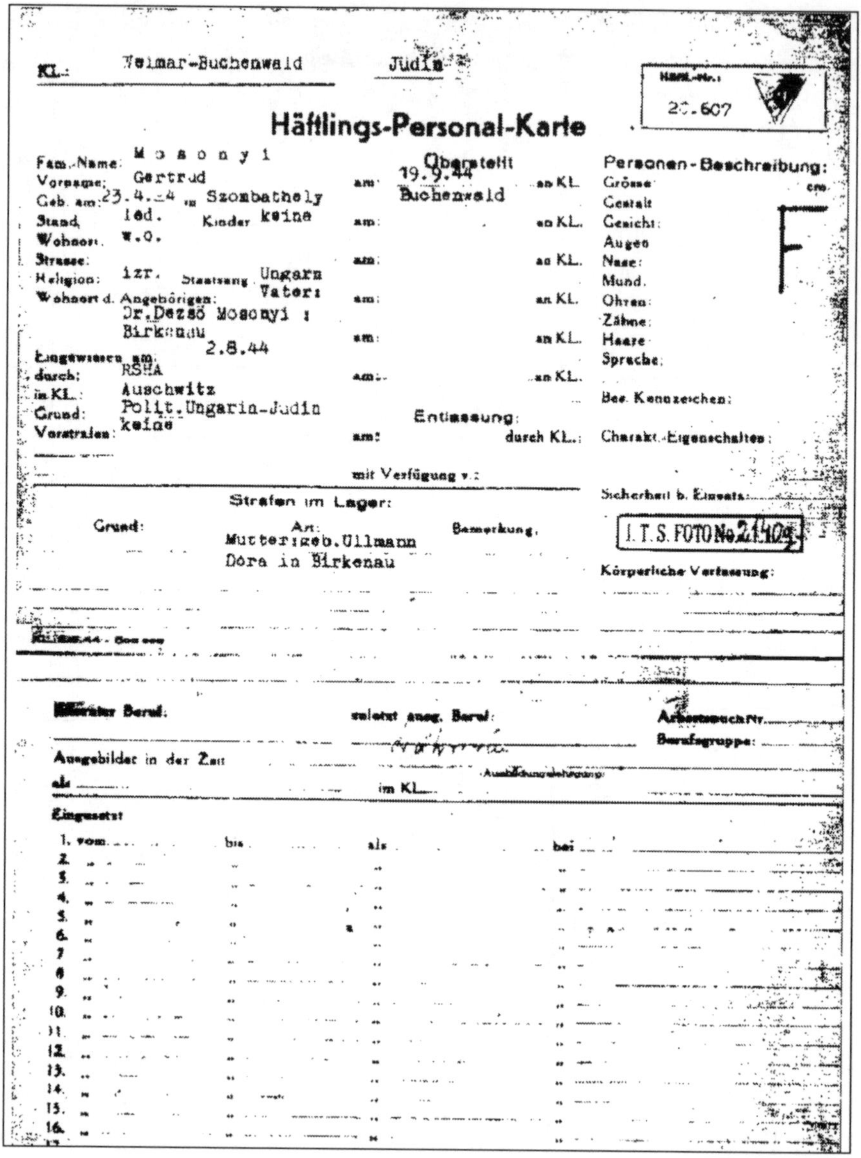

KL.: Weimar-Buchenwald Jüdin

Häftl.-Nr.: 20.607

**Häftlings-Personal-Karte**

Fam.-Name: M o s o n y i
Vorname: Gertrud
Geb. am: 23.4.24 in Szombathely
Stand: led. Kinder: keine
Wohnort: w.o.
Strasse:
Religion: isr. Staatsang.: Ungarn
Wohnort d. Angehörigen: Vater: Dr. Dezsö Mosonyi : Birkenau
Eingewiesen am: 2.8.44
durch: RSHA
im KL.: Auschwitz
Grund: Polit. Ungarin-Jüdin
Vorstrafen: keine

Überstellt am: 19.9.44 an KL. Buchenwald
am: an KL.
am: an KL.
am: an KL.
am: an KL.
am: an KL.

Entlassung:
am: durch KL.:
mit Verfügung v.:

Personen-Beschreibung:
Grösse: cm
Gestalt:
Gesicht:
Augen:
Nase:
Mund:
Ohren:
Zähne:
Haare:
Sprache:
Bes. Kennzeichen:
Charakt.-Eigenschaften:
Sicherheit b. Einsatz:

Strafen im Lager:
Grund: Art: Bemerkung:
Mutter: geb. Ullmann Dora in Birkenau

I.T.S. FOTO No. 2140

Körperliche Verfassung:

Erlernter Beruf: zuletzt ausg. Beruf: Arbeitseinsatz-Nr.: Berufsgruppe:
Ausgebildet in der Zeit als im KL.
Eingesetzt:
1. vom bis als bei
2.
3.
4.
5.
6.
7.
8.
9.
10.
11.
12.
13.
14.
15.
16.

*FIGURE 2: Prisoner's Personal Card: Weimar-Buchenwald Concentration Camp, Gertrud Mosonyi, Jewess. Prisoner Number 20607.*

Sometimes the camp bathroom was closed as a punishment, and I remember this happened once at the beginning of October 1944, when it was snowing outside. I knew that to survive I had to stay healthy, and that meant keeping myself scrupulously clean. That night I risked my life to save my life; I slipped out of the barracks to wash myself down with the fresh snow. It was strictly forbidden to leave the barracks at night, and I could have been shot for it. Luckily, no one noticed.

We also received clothing that nearly fitted, and even underwear. They also gave each of us a piece of cloth, about the size of a brick, printed with our individual prisoner number. We had to sew this onto the back of our clothes to show everybody who we were. We had no faces, no names; we were just numbers. Anybody who didn't like the way I walked or the way I looked could denounce me simply by quoting my number.

\* \* \* \* \*

We had been taken to Hessisch-Lichtenau to work in Hirschhagen munitions factory, which was five and a half kilometres from the camp. Hirschhagen was one of 27 factories owned by Dynamit-Nobel, and this was the second largest in Germany. It was truly vast, two kilometres wide and one kilometre long, with 17 kilometres of railway lines. We were to be used as slave-labourers, helping to make German ammunition. I found out recently that when we arrived in Hessisch-Lichtenau, the foreman from the factory inspected us and said: 'We asked for workers, not skeletons.' This explains why, for the first week, we were given extra food and not made to work at all, so as to build up our strength for work later on.

Our commandant in Hessisch-Lichtenau was a man by the name of Willi Schaefer, who was accompanied everywhere by his beautiful pet dog. Schaefer was not a sadist, but did everything precisely according to the rules. When we arrived at the camp, he told us that if anybody tried to escape, the guards would search for them, and they would be brought back and shot. Some time in September two women did escape, but they were found and brought back to the camp. We had to watch while they were given spades and made to dig their own graves. Then the guards shot them into the pits and we had to bury them. This was how the rules worked.

In Hessisch-Lichtenau we were given a bit more food than in Auschwitz, at least to start with: either a third or a half loaf of bread per day, though this became less and less as time went on. Schaefer himself supervised the bread distribution every day to make sure everybody was given exactly the same amount. He was very strict about nobody getting more than anyone else. We were given bread every day, even if there was hardly any other food. I can only remember two days when we had no bread distribution.

I will come to those two days in a moment, but first I want to describe a special job I did in this camp, and how it possibly saved my life. Some people worked in the kitchens, some worked in the camp, but most of us – including me – became slave-workers in the munitions factory. Factory workers, however, were also made to do odd jobs around camp now and then. Two SS women would come into the room and ask for volunteers, and if you volunteered, there was a chance of getting extra soup afterwards. Even if no soup materialised, the guards would at least treat you decently. If no one offered to do the job, the SS chose people at random and bullied them while they worked. So, though we were weak and exhausted, it was worthwhile volunteering.

One day, at the beginning of October, I volunteered along with a friend of mine. We were taken out of the camp to a place where we saw Commandant Schaefer with his beautiful dog lying dead on the ground by his feet. Our orders were to dig a grave for the dog and bury it. As it had snowed a few days earlier, the ground was frozen and hard. At that point I had dysentery and was in a pretty bad physical state, but nevertheless we dug the grave, with the commandant standing there and watching us the whole time. When we had buried the animal, he actually thanked us politely. From that moment on, whenever he saw me in camp, he greeted me courteously. I had became a person, not just a number, for him.

Our second commandant, Ernst Zorbach, was really the vilest creature – to call him a human being would be impossible; to call him a beast would be an insult to the animal kingdom. He was the vilest creature I have ever come across in my life; an absolute sadist who carried a whip everywhere he went. His greatest pleasure was to hurt people and make them as miserable as possible. He loved for instance to stick our heads into the latrines. Yet Zorbach also appreciated music. The great German poet Goethe once said: 'Evil people have no songs.' But when Zorbach found out that one of the prisoners was a concert pianist, he excused her from work and had a piano brought into camp so that she could practise and he could listen to her. He even organised a concert, which unfortunately I missed, probably because I was on shift work in the factory. So Goethe was wrong – it is possible for evil people to have songs, to love and appreciate music.

I became very friendly with the camp doctor, Luciana Nissim, an Italian Jew and close friend, a fellow student of Primo Levi, one of the most powerful writers on the Holocaust. They had been together in a resistance group in Italy when they were captured and taken to Auschwitz in 1943. She had just finished her medical studies. When our group of Hungarian Jewish women was transferred to Hessisch-Lichtenau, a camp doctor and a nurse were appointed, and Luciana became our doctor. In our group, there was only one woman who spoke Italian and a few who spoke French. Luciana spoke no Hungarian and only sparse German, but was fluent in French. As I could also speak French, we became friends and remained so until 1998, when sadly she died of a brain tumour.

\* \* \* \* \*

As I mentioned earlier, there were two days when we received no bread. In the middle of October, Schaefer was called back to Buchenwald for new orders. While he was away, there was no bread and the prisoners were very angry. We were very hungry, getting weaker and weaker every day. A few days after he returned, I overheard two SS women talking and laughing about the money they had made from selling our bread while Schaefer was away. Then one woman pointed at me and said, 'Sssssh, she might hear us.' The other replied, 'No, she's a complete idiot, she doesn't speak a word of German. I even tried to teach her some words but she can't learn a thing.'

As I explained, I was brought up speaking both German and Hungarian from the earliest age. German was my first language, so of course I understood every word they were saying. But in camp, I had decided not to have any dealings with either the guards or SS women, and pretended to speak no German at all. That day, however, perhaps my expression gave me away – I am not a very good liar. Anyway, the women suspected something. They went into my barrack and asked the first person they came across if it was true that I spoke no German. Unfortunately the inmate they asked was a co-operator, one of those whose only thought was their own survival. She told them right away that I spoke fluent German but refused to communicate in it.

Once the SS women realised I knew they had sold the bread, they tried to bribe me in case I told the commandant and got them into trouble. They offered to make me a work-leader in the factory. Work-leaders had warmer clothing, more food, and were allowed to take the train to work more often than ordinary workers. These extra privileges were very tempting because I was so weak. But work-leaders also had duties. In return for these privileges, I would have had to boss my camp-mates around to make them work harder. I would have been expected to spy on them and denounce them to the guards.

I was only 20 years old and wanted to survive; I didn't want to give the SS the satisfaction of one more Jewish death. But basically, I had a choice: I didn't want to survive at any price. I didn't want to live without my integrity. I told the women I would not be a work-leader. They called me an idiot and told me I was so weak that I would never survive any other way. But I still refused. They stopped trying to persuade me, but before they left, they warned me, 'You're going to pay for this.'

A few days later, the same women came and told me to go to the camp assembly-place. We usually only went there to be counted, and we had already been counted that day, so this was strange. When I arrived, there were lots of women from different barracks gathered there. Then the *Kapo* called the camp doctor and Commandant Schaefer. They counted us, and there were 208 women altogether. This was apparently a problem. What I didn't know then, but found out later from my friend the doctor, was that one of the new orders from Buchenwald was to count how many people had visited the doctor's surgery that week, to see who was expendable. That week, 206 people had visited the surgery. But there were 208 of us standing in the assembly-place.

Willi Schaefer, as I said earlier, did everything precisely according to the rules: the number had to be 206. So, as a document in my possession shows, my deportation number (20,607) was altered and I was taken out of the selection, along with another woman called Weiss. I don't know if it was because Schaefer knew me from when I had buried his dog, or because I had kept my red cheeks and looked healthy, or just pure chance that I escaped. All I know is that I was lucky. The remaining 206 women were taken back to Auschwitz and gassed. We two alone were permitted to go on living.

* * * * *

Our job in Hessisch-Lichtenau was to be slave-workers in the munitions factory, which was two and a half miles away, up a very steep hill. Because we were very weak, it took us about two hours to walk up there. Occasionally we went by train because the German foremen complained that by the time we arrived, we were already exhausted and no use as workers. We worked in three shifts of ten hours each, around the clock, with the first and last hour overlapping with the other groups. It then took us another two hours to get home, so we were out of camp for approximately 14 hours a day, with nothing to eat during that time.

The part of the factory where I worked produced mines and bombs. We were told that we were making grenades, but I found out after the war olitische Abteilung                          Weimar-Buchenwald, 31. Okt. 44

Betrifft: Über teilung von weiblichen Häftlingen vom Akdo
        Hessisch Lichtenau nach dem KL.Auschwitz.

Nach Mitteilung des SS-Kommandos in Hessisch Lichtenau vom 29.10.44
sind die nachstehend aufgeführten Häftlinge am 27.Okt.44 nach dem
KL.Auschwitz zurücküberstellt worden.

### Politische Ungarinnen/Jüdinnen

| Lfde Nr. | Hftl-Nr. | Name | Vorname | Geburtsdatum |
|---|---|---|---|---|
| 1. | 20001 | Adler | Anna | 3.10.20 |
| 2. | 20004 | Adler | Terez | 18. 6.04 |
| 3. | 20005 | Adler | Zelma | 17. 2.02 |
| 4. | 20973 | Almasi | Irma | 22. 8.06 |
| 5. | 20046 | Bartos | Margit | 5. 3.06 |
| 6. | 20045 | Bauer | Iren | 6. 2.10 |
| 7. | 20100 | Baumgatren | Berta | 6. 9.28 |
| 8. | 20101 | Baumgarten | Iren | 14. 8.07 |
| 9. | 20049 | Bender | Eva | 20. 9.12 |
| 10. | 20022 | Bermann | Leontin | 26. 2.05 |
| 11. | 20095 | Birnbaum | Irma | 16.10.15 |
| 12. | 20094 | Birnbaum | Klara | 11. 1.14 |
| 13. | 20097 | Birnbaum | Rossi | 28. 6.25 |
| 14. | 20096 | Birnbaum | Saidonia | 21. 5.27 |
| 15. | 20110 | Biren | Anna | 6. 6.17 |
| 16. | 20028 | Blem | Anna | 22. 8.27 |
| 17 | 20027 | Bloch | Janka | 21.10.03 |
| 18. | 20026 | Bloch | Vera | 22. 8.27 |
| 19. | 20039 | Blosberg | Irene | 7.11.04 |
| 20. | 20119 | Bodi | Anna | 13. 8.25 |
| 21. | 20120 | Bodi | Maria | 4. 1.27 |
| 22. | 20121 | Bodi | Rosie | 9. 4.06 |
| 23. | 20084 | Braun | Eva | 20.12.07 |
| 24. | 20088 | Braun | Klara | 5. 2.26 |
| 25. | 20102 | Breiner | Lenke | 26. 1.05 |
| 26. | 20041 | Bruckner | Elsa | 6. 7.04 |
| 27. | 20042 | Burger | Györgyi | 24. 4.21 |
| 28. | 20138 | Csöban | Jolan | 15.10.12 |
| 29. | 20155 | Deutsch | Aranka | 27.12.00 |
| 30. | 20146 | Deutsch | Edith | 14. 5.22 |
| 31. | 20147 | Deutsch | Erzsebet | 3.12.24 |
| 32. | 20144 | Deutsch | Ibolya | 15. 8.26 |
| 33. | 20154 | Deutsch | Ilona | 14. 3.09 |
| 34. | 20152 | Deutsch | Sari | 9. 5.05 |
| 35. | 20148 | Deutsch | Selma | 15. 5.14 |
| 36. | 20156 | Deutschmann | Gizella | 29. 1.25 |
| 37. | 20141 | Donnenberg | Janka | 17. 4.01 |
| 38. | 20176 | Eisenreich | Agnes | 13. 8.25 |
| 39. | 20177 | Eisenreich | Klara | 13. 8.25 |
| 40. | 20175 | Eisenreich | Magda | 9. 5.24 |
| 41. | 20178 | Erdös | Jolán | 15. 2.05 |
| 42. | 20202 | Fabian | Olga | 5. 8.08 |
| 43. | 20186 | Farkas | Rachel | 17. 2.02 |
| 44. | 20195 | Fein | Edith | 25.11.21 |
| 45. | 20223 | Fellner | Ilonka | 29. 7.22 |

*Dokument 19b*
*Die Namen der Frauen, die aus Hess. Lichtenau zum KZ Auschwitz-Birkenau „überstellt" wurden. (Dokument 19b–19e)*

FIGURE 3: *Document showing the transfer of female prisoners from Hessisch-Lichtenau back to Auschwitz, 29 October 1944. Trude's prisoner number, 20607, was originally on the list, but her number was changed and she was removed from the selection.*
*Taken from Dieter Vaupel,* Spuren die nicht vergehen [Traces which do not Disappear] *(Kassel: Verlag Gesamthochschul-Bibliothek, 2001). Dokument 19b–19c, pp.84–7.*

## Politische Ungarinnen/Jüdinnen

| Lfde Nr. | Hftl-Nr. | Name | Vorname | Geburtsdatum |
|---|---|---|---|---|
| | | — 3.— | | 31. Okt. 1944 |
| 106. | 20428 | Klein | Zsuzsanna | 21. 3.21 |
| 107. | 20478 | Knapp | Anna | 2. 8.10 |
| 108. | 20465 | Knöpfler | Kata | 1. 7.23 |
| 109. | 20464 | Knöpfker | Margit | 16. 5.00 |
| 110. | 20466 | Knöpfler | Rozsi | 6. 4.25 |
| 111. | 20496 | Koch | Irma | 11.10.15 |
| 112. | 20476 | Kovacs | Eszter | 16. 3.25 |
| 113. | 20474 | Kraj | Erzsebet | 5. 9.10 |
| 114. | 20475 | Kraj | Jolan | 17.11.12 |
| 115. | 20473 | Krämer | Bella | 13. 3.06 |
| 116. | 20472 | Krämer | Rosa | 28.10.24 |
| 117. | 20471 | Kromovits | Iren | 24. 7.18 |
| 118. | 20470 | Kromovits | Rozsi | 13. 1.20 |
| 119. | 20481 | Kirschner | Gitte | 30. 8.03 |
| 120. | 20722 | Lackenbach | Etel | 17. 2.06 |
| 121. | 20543 | Latzer | Maria | 6. 1.00 |
| 122. | 20546 | Lebovits | Maria | 25. 8.1a |
| 123. | 20509 | Leicht | Relli | 15. 2.07 |
| 124. | 20533 | Lusztig | Berta | 10.10.01 |
| 125. | 20985 | Lusztig | Iren | 27. 4.00 |
| 126. | 20576 | Mayersberg | Terez | 20. 7.08 |
| 127. | 20553 | Molnar | Magdalena | 10. 2.18 |
| 128. | 20564 | Morvai | Aranka | 19.11.07 |
| 129. | 20565 | Morvai | Lenke | 14.12.06 |
| 130. | 20598 | Moskovits | Erzsebet | 14.11.14 |
| 131. | 20607 ol | Moskovits | Hajnal | 20. 2.26 |
| 132. | 20615 | Neumann | Jozsa | 28.11.11 |
| 133. | 20656 | Paskesz | Seren | 27. 8.21 |
| 134. | 20657 | Pfeifer | Magda | 4. 8.08 |
| 135. | 20658 | Polgar | Ilona | 3. 7.05 |
| 136. | 20661 | Politzer | Iren | 27.10.07 |
| 137. | 20627 | Pollak | Berta | 12. 7.04 |
| 138. | 20988 | Pollak | Erzsebet | 24.10.05 |
| 139. | 20626 | Pollak | Magda | 26.11.22 |
| 140. | 20710 | Rado | Agnes | 9. 8.24 |
| 141. | 20699 | Ramar | Edith | 5.12.24 |
| 142. | 20689 | Reimar | Lilla | 28. 1.24 |
| 143. | 20668 | Reinitz | Franciska | 6. 8.06 |
| 144. | 20703 | Reisz | Gisella | 12. 7.05 |
| 145. | 20690 | Rendel | Erzsebet | 23. 4.22 |
| 146. | 20712 | Resovszky | Klara | 23. 1.20 |
| 147. | 20682 | Rintel | Karolin | 9. 2.04 |
| 148. | 20681 | Rintel | Veronika | 18. 1.26 |
| 149. | 20702 | Roman | Ella | 13.12.02 |
| 150. | 20696 | Rosenberg | Hilda | 19. 4.17 |
| 151. | 20694 | Rosenberg | Margit | 16. 3.20 |
| 152. | 20716 | Rosenberger | Katalin | 3. 9.05 |
| 153. | 20717 | Rosenfeld | Erzsebet | 3. 3.09 |
| 154. | 20718 | Rosenfeld | Zseni | 6. 9.05 |
| 155. | 20700 | Roskovits | Etel | 27. 1.11 |
| 156. | 20709 | Rosmann | Margit | 14. 6.06 |
| 157. | 20692 | Rivel | Helen | 26. 5.14 |
| 158. | 20780 | Seidmann | Gisella | 10. 7.21 |
| 159. | 20733 | Singer | Gisella | 16.12.10 |
| 160. | 20777 | Singer | Ibit | 28. 3.29 |
| 161. | 20636 | Smil | Mili | 3. 2.23 |
| 162. | 20829 | Smuk | Elisabeta | 21. 5.24 |
| 163. | 20827 | Smuk | Ilona | 18. 2.05 |
| 164. | 20828 | Smuk | Malvin | 18. 8.07 |
| 165. | 20846 | Sommer | Regina | 17.11.00 |

**Dokument 8d**

*FIGURE 3: Continued*

Politische Ungarinnen/Jüdinnen

| Lfde Nr. | Hftl- Nr. | Name | Vorname | Geburtsdatum |
|---|---|---|---|---|
| 167. | 20791 | Schäfer | | |
| 168. | 20771 | Schick | | |
| 169. | 20772 | Schick | | |
| 170. | 20769 | Schick | | |
| 171. | 20770 | Schick | | |
| 172. | 20779 | Schlesinge | | |
| 173. | 20787 | Schlesinge | | |
| 174. | 20750 | Schwarcz | | |
| 175. | 20755 | Schwarcz | | |
| 176. | 20745 | Schwartz | | |
| 177. | 20749 | Schwartz | | |
| 178. | 20833 | Stein | | |
| 179. | 20803 | Steiner | | |
| 180. | 20804 | Steiner | | |
| 181. | 20802 | Steiner | | |
| 182. | 20818 | Stern | | |
| 183. | 20783 | Strasser | | |
| 184. | 20721 | Strauber | | |
| 185. | 20869 | Ulmann | | |
| 186. | 20880 | Vajda | | |
| 187. | 20879 | Vajda | | |
| 188. | 20877 | Wachsler | | |
| 189. | 20878 | Wachsler | | |
| 190. | 20922 | Weil | | |
| 191. | 20931 | Weiler | | |
| 192. | 20954 | Weiser | | |
| 193. | 20919 | Weiss | | |
| 194. | 20998 02 | Weiss | | |
| 195. | 20897 | Weiss | | |
| 196. | 20909 | Weiss | | |
| 197. | 20896 | Weiss | | |
| 198. | 20900 | Weiss | | |
| 199. | 20944 | Weitmann | | |
| 200. | 20945 | Weitmann | | |
| 201. | 20881 | Weltinger | | |
| 202. | 20953 | Winter | | |
| 203. | 20887 | Wollak | | |
| 204. | 20967 | Zsigmond | | |
| 205. | 20968 | Zsigmond | | |
| 206. | 20969 | Zsigmond | | |

Listenstärke : 206 Häftlinge

FIGURE 3: Continued

that they were actually German flying bombs. They were pear-shaped with a round rod and seven wings, and our job was to assemble them and fill the bottom part with explosives. When we had arrived in the camp, the SS guards had noted down on their papers if we had a profession, if we were housewives, students, or whatever. In our group there were a number of chemists, and the Germans made the very silly mistake of letting the chemists mix the explosives for the bombs. It did not occur to them that they would know how to render the explosives useless! This was wonderful since some of us had decided that we didn't want to help the German war effort at all, and would rather spend our time disabling the bombs than making them.

We very carefully gathered together a small sabotage group. Supervision was very strict, so we had to find a way of getting round it, and what we did was initially to double our production rate. The German foremen must then have thought, 'These stupid Jewish women think that if they work like mad, they are more likely to survive. So we don't need to supervise them that much.' The supervision became very lax. Without delay, we set to work.

The chemists worked out how to change the explosive mixture and whenever they were not supervised, they would fill the bombs with the dud mixture instead. The scientists who worked with these explosives in the mixing or filling rooms often developed yellow skin and were called the 'canaries'. Very often they were completely poisoned by the chemicals used in the explosive. After a while, they would be in terrible pain and have to go into the sick bay, where a 'canary' would scream day and night for four or five days. When the screaming stopped, you knew that there was one 'canary' less.

I was not a chemist, but nonetheless I did what I could to help the sabotage effort. My first job was on a conveyor belt and all I had to do – it was a very easy job – was sit there working on the bombs as they came past. I had to take two caps made of Bakelite (similar to today's plastic), and screw them on tightly. If there was no supervision, I put the caps on the slant or just pretended to screw them on so they could easily be damaged in the offloading bay. After a little while, I realised that sitting at a conveyor belt for ten hours a day every day would drive me mad, so the next time the foreman asked for a volunteer for a new job, without telling us what it would be, I put myself forward and became the 'horse'.

The job of the 'horse', as you might expect, was to pull a cart. At the end of the conveyor belt, I had to load 40 bombs in a pyramid onto a four-wheeled flat iron trolley. The bombs weighed 25 kilograms each and I had to lift two at a time, hooking the wings together. It was very difficult work, and I damaged a nail and a toe by accidentally dropping bombs onto them; the toe was later amputated. I had to wheel the trolley through a heavy iron door and get it onto rails which were at the top of a steep hill; then I had to guide the trolley slowly down the hill while someone else stood at the back working the trolley's brake. The offloading bay was at the bottom of the hill and the bombs were unloaded there ready to be taken away. As there was practically never any supervision, I always tried to knock the caps off and bend the wings. Hopefully it did some damage. Then I had to pull the trolley back up to the top and load it all over again.

The hill was extremely steep. Sometimes it was very dangerous, especially if it rained or snowed, because the rails were very slippery. As I was barefoot or in clogs, I couldn't get much grip on the ground and had to rely on the person who worked the brake to stop the trolley from running away. Unfortunately, some of my workmates were not very good at this, and it then became really perilous work because I could easily have been squashed between the trolley and the door of the offloading bay.

At first I was lucky because there was a German worker operating the brakes. Whenever he worked with me, I had no need at all to be afraid, because I knew he would be looking after me. He was a Communist and was opposed to everything that Hitler stood for. Though we were not supposed to speak to each other, we managed to communicate from time to time. He had seven children but was very poor and had great difficulty supporting his family.

Sometimes, usually on the night shift, he would bring me a tiny piece of bread or a little onion wrapped in a piece of newspaper, and he would say: 'Go into the corner and eat it, then give me the paper back.' The paper always contained a report about the Germans being defeated, to give me and my fellow prisoners hope that the war would soon be over. Unfortunately, this German disappeared quite soon because he was caught helping one of the slave-labourers, and transferred elsewhere. After the war, I tried to find out who he was because his help meant so much to me. Sadly, I had partial amnesia afterwards and one of the things I could not remember was his name. I would have loved to thank him because the smallest gesture of humanity meant so much to us under those circumstances. But I never managed to remember his name or find it out from anyone else. I am also still trying to discover the names of the two SS women who tried to send me back to Auschwitz, but have been unsuccessful as yet. But when I talk about this German worker, I feel that I am at least giving thanks to his memory.

At Christmas we heard American planes bombing Kassel, 27 kilometres from camp, and people thought we would be liberated very soon;

but they were wrong. Though Kassel was practically razed to the ground, the factory, which could not have been camouflaged, was never bombed. In fact the Allies knew for certain that there was a munitions factory there, because it had been photographed from the air. We remained in Hessisch-Lichtenau until the end of March; when the factory ran out of material our camp was evacuated. As the food supplies had decreased constantly during our internment there, we had been getting weaker all the time.

\* \* \* \* \*

The guards loaded us onto a train and we set off amidst rumours that they were taking us to Buchenwald to be killed. Then an American plane bombed the engine and our carriage remained stationary on the railway tracks for three days before another one arrived. The train did not head for Buchenwald, probably because by that time the American army was approaching and the camp was liberated a few days later. Instead, we were taken back East, to Leipzig.

The first place we went to was a well-equipped camp called Leipzig-Schoenau, in the town of Leipzig itself. I remember it had clean bunks and bed linen, and hot showers, and we were even given a proper meal. We couldn't understand why we had been taken there. Next morning the camp was bombed. Until a few days earlier, it had actually been SS accommodation, which explains why it was so luxurious. The Americans must have thought the SS were still there and were trying to bomb them. My best friend was killed during that raid; her head was split in half and I was holding her hand at the time.

Next, we were marched through the burning city to another camp outside Leipzig called Tekla. It was still snowing and I was barefoot and wearing only a sleeveless flannel shirt. Tekla had 15,000 inmates, men and women; there were Jews, prisoners-of-war and various other groups. We stayed there for five days, from 7 to 12 April 1945. We were not supposed to speak to the men in the camp and were separated from them by barbed wire, but I did anyway. A French inmate gave me a threadbare striped jacket and a piece of soap.

On 12 April 1945 we were taken out of Tekla to begin a forced death-march. We marched in rows of five, pulling the German guards' luggage on wooden trolleys. We were given nothing to eat and slept on frozen ground. Anyone who collapsed along the way or could not get up in the morning was shot on the spot. The guards told us they were taking us to Dresden, but instead they took us to the River Elbe. We marched round and round six times in an elliptical circle, walking through the same villages, from one side of the river to the other. Each time round, there were fewer of us left because people collapsed and were shot along the way. During those ten days, the Americans were moving in from the West and the Russians from the East. When we were on the American side, a small American plane often flew overhead. If the Americans saw a German uniform, they would shoot at it, so the German guards wore striped concentration camp jackets over their uniforms to disguise themselves as prisoners.

On the last night, 22 April, we were on the Russian side of the River Elbe in a forest clearing. A Russian plane circled round us and fired a few shots, but not at us. For the first time in ten days, we were given something to eat. The guards slaughtered a horse in front of us and threw pieces of raw horsemeat at us, as though we were dogs. We also had to queue up for a handful of uncooked rice, which we couldn't really eat: because of malnutrition we had lost many of our teeth. By this time, I had dysentery again and was extremely weak.

That night we slept in the clearing and were woken very early in the morning while it was still dark. I think the guards must have realised they were going to be captured and thought they would rather fall into American than Russian hands. They decided to head for the American side of the river as soon as they could. As we came to the bridge over the Elbe, I could barely carry on. When we got onto the bridge, the sun started to come up over the horizon and as we crossed, there was the most beautiful sunrise I have ever seen, before or since.

By the time we reached the other side, the sun was up and I collapsed. I knew it was the end for me; I didn't care any more; I was much too weak to mind. Two guards came and shouted at me to get up, but I could not. They butted me with their guns and then one of them said, 'Oh, leave her, she isn't worth a bullet any more.' They walked away to chase those who were still on their feet. That is why I lived to tell my story.

* * * * *

After the guards abandoned me at the side of the road, I felt extremely cold. I saw a wooden building very nearby and dragged myself inside with great difficulty: I was too weak even to sit upright. A German girl found me and warned me it would be dangerous to stay there; it was a stable for horses belonging to German soldiers who were still in the area. She advised me to move into the neighbouring barn, and also gave me a nice chunk of bread.

In the barn I met two of my camp-mates who had managed to escape from the death-march during the night. Later that night, we were discovered by Russian prisoners-of-war who were looking for farmers who had ill-treated them. They had since rejoined the Russian Army and now wanted revenge. They must have been disappointed because all they found was three starving women. They took us into the farm and early next morning when they set off to rejoin the other soldiers, they took the other two women with them, saying they would be repatriated to Hungary. I refused to accompany them. I had already decided not to return there.

Later on, I heard French being spoken outside. I dragged myself to the window and saw ten French prisoners-of-war washing in the courtyard. As I spoke French, I introduced myself to them and they told me they were going to a place called Wurzen, 29 kilometres away, where there was an American liberation centre. They invited me to join them, but I was still too weak even to sit up, so naturally I was unable to go with them. The Frenchmen then left, but one of them, Charles, came back to say that he would take care of me until I was able to walk. He was very kind to me and within a few days I fell in love with him. He felt the same about me, or so he said, and asked me to marry him and go with him to France.

From my early childhood, I had always been a complete Francophile. The French language sounded so beautiful to me that I would listen to it on the radio like music. My aunt had married a Frenchman, my adored godfather. Budapest itself was known as 'Little Paris' and many Hungarian painters, writers, and poets spent time in France, so it is not surprising that I was excited by the idea of going there. Charles was no intellectual but he was kind and good to me. I was extremely happy – I was free and in love, and I was going to France, the land of my dreams.

When I was well enough, we set off for Wurzen, and on the way there we had a stroke of luck. Two open lorries pulled by a tractor flying a French flag took us to the liberation centre. There were 40 passengers on the lorries when we arrived and the 11 women in the group were all concentration camp survivors. The men were a mixed lot, some prisoners-of-war, some camp survivors. As we were an organised group with transport, the American authorities issued us with vouchers for food and lodging, and after a day in the liberation centre, we were allowed to proceed to the French border.

In a few days' time, our group reached Metz, the French liberation centre. We were in fact the first concentration camp survivors to reach France. We were fêted, given food, money and clothing, and sent on to Paris. Although my French godfather was living in Paris at the time, I had partial amnesia and could remember no names at all, so I could not find him. It turned out later that he was living in the next street to where we were staying! From Paris, we made our way slowly towards Charles's home town of Toulon. At every stage we were inundated with presents, and by the time we arrived, I had six or seven suitcases full of food and clothing and quite a lot of money.

At the Red Cross station in Toulon, we were cross-examined by the authorities. After a while, Charles told them that as he hadn't seen his mother for five years and she didn't even know he was alive, he thought it would be better if he went home and then came back for me. He did not return, and the police had to oblige him to come back for me. I had only been admitted to France because he had told all the authorities that he was going to marry me and signed the relevant document.

Charles's family lived in a flat on the third floor. In the kitchen there was a curtain hiding the two buckets that were emptied through the window into the courtyard. Charles's mother and his very attractive, blonde 16-year-old sister were obviously not best pleased with the gift he had brought them from the war; they made it clear that I was not welcome. I had to share a bed with his sister. But I tried to be as helpful as possible. Even though the circumstances were not quite what I had imagined, I was still happy. The only problem was that Charles had disappeared again and I was left with the women.

In the evening, the women dressed up in their finery and took me to an open-air bar in the port. I was enchanted; it was like a scene from the French films I had loved so much. The bar was lit with coloured bulbs and filled with sailors, Frenchmen, Chinese, black men. I was fascinated. Men came up and asked us to dance. Although the other two danced, I refused. I would not dance with anyone but Charles, nor would I drink if he was not there. Again and again the women vanished, leaving me sitting by myself. It took me three days to realise why they were getting nastier and nastier to me. They were prostitutes, and I was expected to join them.

I then insisted that I wanted to see Charles, and when he reappeared two days later, I asked him to take me to the Red Cross station. I thought that as a qualified nursery nurse and nursery school teacher, who also spoke French, it would be easy for me to get a job. Charles told me to go to the station wearing my concentration camp clothing, my grey sleeveless flannel shirt and my threadbare grey and blue striped jacket, leaving all my possessions behind in his home. He would bring them to me once I had settled somewhere.

Outside the station he told me to wait while he checked if the Red Cross officials were there. A few minutes later, he appeared with two policemen who handcuffed me and threw me into a tiny cell. The shock caused my memory to return, but it also sent me into deep despair. I decided that if this was my fate after being in concentration camp, I did not want to go on living. I found a piece of glass and tried to slit my wrists, but the glass was thick and it was a very slow job. I still have a small scar on my wrist today.

Before I had managed to kill myself, I was taken into the office for interrogation. It turned out that Charles had lied to the police that he had discovered I was an ex-SS German woman and he was therefore unable to marry me. It was difficult for me to prove my story as I had no papers, and in the camps our group had never been tattooed so there was no number on my arm. Because I always had red cheeks, I looked healthy even when I was ill. In addition, after being liberated I had developed a condition called *anémie graisseuse,* and had put on a lot of weight very quickly; within weeks I had gone from 38 kilograms, my weight on arrival in Wurzen, to 98 kilograms. However, the shock of being locked up jolted my memory and I suddenly remembered names. To convince them, I gave them all the names I could remember: my godfather in Paris, my aunt in New York, my mother's cousin in Switzerland and the name of a French worker in the off-loading hall of the munitions factory, Paul Morell from Bordeaux.

From the prison in Toulon, I was transferred to a town called Bandol where I was imprisoned alongside French and Italian Fascists and German SS women. Three weeks later, I was sent to the Prison St Pierre in Marseilles. By the time we arrived there, all the people I had named to the police had replied verifying the facts I gave. The prison authorities knew that my story was true, but could not release me until my file arrived from Toulon. However, the prefect of Toulon had lost two sons in the resistance, and did not believe my story. He refused to give my file to the authorities in Marseilles, so I remained in prison for four and a half months.

Finally, I was liberated and after spending two weeks in a deportees' convalescent home in Marseilles, I went back to Paris. I never saw Charles or any of my gifts again, and had only the clothes on my back. The prison authorities apologised for my wrongful imprisonment, but never gave me any compensation.

* * * * *

My parents did not survive the Holocaust, and most of my childhood friends were also exterminated. I use this word knowingly because Jews and Gypsies were considered vermin, and vermin is exterminated in preference by gas. My grandmother was taken to Theresienstadt concentration camp after the *Anschluss,* the annexation of Austria, and from there to

Auschwitz, where she was murdered. My other grandmother, who was in Budapest, first went into hiding with one of her grandsons. Then they ran out of food and he took her into the ghetto. However, it wasn't much better there; when the war ended, her grandson went to fetch her back. He had to take her home in a wheelbarrow; she was so weak from starvation that she could not walk and died a few days later.

There was nothing left for me in Hungary and I decided not to go back there. As a result I lost my citizenship and became stateless. Until 1957 I was a wandering Jew, an asylum-seeker, often working illegally in order to survive. I know what it means to be an asylum-seeker and I feel great sympathy for today's refugees. From Paris I eventually made my way in 1948 to South Africa using a false Hungarian passport, which was taken away from me as soon as it expired. I was told that I was not to consider myself Hungarian.

In 1957, I became a South African citizen. South Africa was a beautiful country but because of apartheid – introduced a week after my arrival in 1948 by the then government – black people were all second-class citizens. They were exploited and not given the chance of proper education. I hate injustice and usually speak out against it, but I could not say anything. Had I done so, I would not have been able to get that vital piece of paper – a passport and a new nationality. I did not want to stay in South Africa, but was unable to leave until I had proper papers. So I had to keep quiet and hated it. I had to accept that speaking out would not have helped anyone, and it would certainly have harmed me.

Four days after my South African passport finally arrived, I was on a ship to England. I then received British citizenship in 1958 and had full civil rights for the first time in my life. The day I collapsed on the death-march, 23 April 1945, was my twenty-first birthday. It had taken 13 more years before I regained the rights of a citizen of a free country, and was accepted as a complete human being with full civil rights again.

# CHAPTER 3

# *Questions and Answers*

*How did your parents explain to you about anti-Semitism? (18-year-old, Germany)*

When I was a little girl, my father, who was a doctor, used to take me for a walk every Sunday morning. I was always dressed up in my Sunday best, a lovely red coat, white lacy socks and black patent-leather shoes. One Sunday morning when I was five years old, he told me that the previous night he had attended the birth of a baby and wanted to check up on it, so we would go and see the family before the rest of our walk.

We went to a part of the town that I had never seen before. I waited in a large, desolate courtyard surrounded by terraced houses while my father attended his patient. All around me were houses with one narrow door and a narrow window. I saw curtains twitching at the windows. One door opened and then another, and suddenly the courtyard was full of children. They called me a 'dirty Jewish pig' and pelted me with stones until I was bleeding and crying with the shock. When my father came back, they ran away.

I remember telling my father that I was not dirty because I had had a bath that day, and that a pig was a kind of animal but I was a girl. And what did 'Jewish' mean? My family was not religious, so I had not heard the word before. My father told me about minorities and that the Jews were considered a minority. He explained that some people liked to attack weaker people to make themselves feel more powerful, and so the Jews were often hurt. This was the first time I had ever heard of anti-Semitism. I remember clearly that I said to him, 'Alright, from now on I am going to be a Jew.'

## How did it feel to be a member of the Jewish community between 1938 and 1944? (13-year-old, England)

First of all, I should mention that my family was more or less atheist; they did not go to synagogue and attend services or perform any Jewish rituals. I had to attend religious education at school because it was a compulsory subject in Hungary. I hated it, probably mainly because I hated my teacher. He targeted and punished me physically because he disliked my family.

When I was about 14, I went through a religious phase. I took religion so seriously that when I realised that synagogue was the only place we were allowed to meet boys, I felt it was not reverent to use the synagogue for this purpose and stopped attending. I was an odd person with many principles.

However, I always accepted being Jewish. Because Hungary was quite an anti-Semitic country and the Hungarians themselves introduced many anti-Jewish laws independently of Hitler, I felt like the captain of a sinking ship who refuses to abandon his vessel. At the age of nine I became a Zionist and believed that there should be a Jewish state.

There were many restrictions imposed on Jews in Hungary during the 1940s, including a *Numerus Clausus* limiting the number of Jews allowed to enter schools, universities, the civil service and the army. The regime in Hungary co-operated with Hitler, although its leader, Miklós Horthy, did prevent the country's Jews from being deported until 1944. But he allowed the Nazis to deport all the Jews who lived in Hungary, who were not Hungarian. Many Jews were taken from the territories that Hitler returned to Hungary in 1941 and 1942 – from Slovakia, the Carpathians, Yugoslavia, Transylvania and other places.

The town where we lived, Szombathely, was highly anti-Semitic. Ferenc Szálasi, the head of the Arrow Cross (the Hungarian Fascist Party), had a very big following among the people who lived there, and it was one of his favourite towns. Szombathely was also an extremely Catholic place with a very beautiful bishop's palace in the town, and a history of intolerance. Until, I believe, 1860, only Catholics were allowed to sleep in the town or stay there after 6 p.m.

Let me give you some examples of the anti-Semitism we experienced. My father was a founding member of the town's orchestra, but was thrown out for being Jewish, along with all the other Jewish members. One of my uncles married a Christian woman, and their daughter was brought up as a Christian, knowing nothing of Judaism. But she was still deported to Auschwitz because the Nazis considered her racially impure. When I met her in Auschwitz, she was much more lost than me because she didn't understand why she was there. Psychologically, she suffered even more than I did.

My father was a gynaecologist, but also worked as a doctor on the railways. In 1942 he was told that unless he converted to Christianity and was baptised, he would lose his job. He was an atheist and refused to be baptised, feeling it would be wrong to misuse any religion. A colleague of his, a practising Jew, was baptised, together with his family. It was a foolish move on his part because the other Jews despised him and the Christians did not accept him for what he had done, and he was fired four months later anyway. The Church did not protect him. He and his family were killed in Auschwitz just like my parents.

### Did you feel lucky for the first five years of the war because the Nazis had not captured you? (14-year-old, England)

We were not actually occupied until 1944, but in 1941 the German army spent three days in my home town of Szombathely, on its way to Yugoslavia. During those days, there was a curfew and Jewish people were not permitted to go outside after 6 p.m. We were also forbidden to visit the market before 10 a.m., which was very bad because in those days we bought all our vegetables, fruit and fish from there, and after 10 a.m. there was only rubbish left that no one else would buy. And many Jewish people were attacked.

It gave us a foretaste of things to come. We did not know how long the army was going to stay, and after they left, the restrictions continued in our town for a long time – as far as I know, it was the only Hungarian town where these restrictions existed. For those three days, our town was actually occupied, so we were certainly grateful that at least it was not a continual occupation until March 1944.

*How did you feel when you had to put on the yellow star? (17-year-old, Germany)*

We were very frightened. We knew that Jews were being beaten up and dragged away, and no one knew where they had disappeared to. I only left the house when I absolutely had to. It was particularly bad in Hungary because there was such widespread anti-Semitism.

*How come you were not put into a camp until 1944? (15-year-old, England)*

At the beginning of 1944, we thought the war was nearly over and the Germans would surrender quite soon. However, Hungary was occupied on 19 March 1944, and things happened swiftly after that. Adolf Eichmann, a high-ranking Nazi, was in charge of organising the deportations. He must have had the names of all the Hungarian Jews prepared and ready. Within seven and a half weeks all the Hungarian provinces were emptied of Jews, around 430,000 people. Ninety per cent of the Hungarian Jews taken to Auschwitz were gassed immediately. Only the young and strong were given the chance of survival.

I was spared because I was only 20 years old. The Nazis needed the able-bodied for slave-labour in factories making munitions and other goods. A slave-labourer's average life-span was calculated at just nine months. I worked as a slave-labourer for eight and a half months, so I was even luckier to survive.

*What sort of camp were you in? (14-year-old, England)*

The first camp I experienced was Auschwitz-Birkenau, which was all three types in one: extermination, labour and concentration camp. Since I looked young and strong enough to become a slave-labourer (otherwise I would have been killed straight away), I was transferred after four weeks to the control of Buchenwald concentration camp and put into an out-camp called Hessisch-Lichtenau to work in the munitions factory there.

When the factory closed down at the end of March 1945, we were evacuated to a former SS camp called Schoenau in Leipzig, which was bombed by the Americans on the day after we arrived. We then spent five days in another concentration camp called Tekla, before having to go on the death-march.

*What did the guards say to you when they put you on the train to the camp? (14-year-old, England)*

'Hurry up! Get in quickly!' [*Schnell, schnell, 'rein!*] and then they pushed us roughly into the cattle-trucks.

*What sort of work did you have to do in the camps? (13-year-old, England)*

In Auschwitz we didn't have to do any work, we just tried to stay alive. In Hessisch-Lichtenau, we worked in the munitions factory producing flying bombs. I was in a sabotage group and did all I could to ensure that the bombs that passed through my hands would not work properly.

Work in the camp itself could be anything: cleaning the toilets, carrying heavy loads of timber or stone, or helping in the kitchens (I was never lucky enough to do that). There were odd jobs too, like once when I had to dig a grave for the commandant's dead dog.

*What were the beds like, if there were any? (14-year-old, England)*

In Auschwitz we slept sitting up on the bare powdery earth, without even enough space to lie out flat. We sat back-to-back, all cramped together. In the second camp I was in, Hessisch-Lichtenau, there were two-tier bunks. We all had a sack filled with dry straw to serve as a mattress, but it was full of bugs that ate us alive at night. We also had a very rough blanket, but there were no sheets or pillows.

*What, and when, did you eat on an average day? (14-year-old, England)*

In Auschwitz, we had watery coffee in the mornings, and for lunch there was thin soup to drink, then bread and a piece of sausage, or quite a large piece of tasty, but rather salty cheese. That was all we were given in 24 hours. We were very thirsty all the time because it was a hot summer and there was no access to water. Although the cheese made us even thirstier, it was the only real food we got, so I always ate my bread and cheese right away so that no one could take it away from me. What one has, one has!

Later, in the labour camp at Hessisch-Lichtenau, we had quite a bit to eat at first, although for 14 hours a day we had no food as we were working in the factory. There was bread, but less and less of it as time went on. Usually we had soup, and I think there were some potatoes, carrots, cabbage, or other seasonal vegetables. We were also given a little bit of margarine and some jam. The only place to keep food was in the small bowl (or cup or mug) we were given, which we would put at the foot of our bed. This bowl was usually full of bedbugs, but we were so hungry that we ate the food anyway, bugs and all. I remember very little about the food, only that we received less and less, and got hungrier and hungrier, as time went on.

At the end of March 1945, we were put onto our death-march and went without food for ten or eleven days. We were already extremely weak and very hungry. Many people collapsed from hunger and exhaustion along the way and were shot on the spot. I must have weighed approximately 35 kilograms (four and a half stone) when I collapsed and the guards decided I was not even worth a bullet. But it was the fact that I looked so emaciated and thin which saved me.

### Did you ever get close to the gas chambers and furnace? (14-year-old, England)

No. I only saw on arrival the chimneys and pinkish-yellowish smoke and smelt the stench of the burning bodies.

### Were you able to perform any religious festivals in the camps? (14-year-old, England)

I myself was not religious or traditional and did not care about the festivals. Some people did try to light a candle if they were able somehow to lay their hands on one. Or else they burned their margarine ration, if there was one, as though it were a candle. They would fast on Yom Kippur, the Jewish fast day, when one is supposed to eat nothing for 24 hours.

I could not understand why they did it, because in Jewish law the most important law is to sustain life. As we were starving, they would have been excused from fasting. But then everyone had to do what seemed right to them. I suppose that in a way I respected such people for keeping their faith so strong, even in those horrific circumstances.

## *How did you celebrate Passover? (14-year-old, England)*

Before the deportation, my family usually went to another house to celebrate Passover; we didn't really observe Jewish festivals at home. In camp it was more or less impossible to celebrate Passover rituals properly, since there was hardly any food, and certainly none of the unleavened bread and extra plates which were required. Even the ultra-religious could only celebrate by saying their prayers. For the eight days of Passover, some of them did not even eat the little bread we received, because you were not supposed to eat leavened bread. But it didn't really concern me.

## *Did you ever feel that you were missing out on days like birthdays and Christmas? (14-year-old, England)*

Well, not really. I was at home with my mother on my twentieth birthday and as my father had just been deported, we were not thinking about my birthday. My twenty-first birthday was the day I collapsed on the death-march. I should have been shot on the spot like all the others who fell to the ground, but the guards left me there to die. That was the best birthday present I was ever given.

As for Christmas, it was a Christian holiday. When I was small, we did have a Christmas tree and because all the cousins on my father's side were Christian, we celebrated with them. I loved the lights, the smell of a real Christmas tree and the candles, and I relished all the special Christmas food. In Hungary there was a kind of cake called *beugli*, a thin pastry rolled up and filled with either poppy-seed or a walnut mixture. All the housewives competed to make the best cake. But basically it was not my festival; I was, and felt, Jewish, and Christmas was certainly of no religious significance to me.

## *Did you keep a diary of your thoughts and feelings? (13-year-old, England)*

I regret that I didn't. It was difficult to obtain paper or pencil, or to find time to write, and perhaps I was too tired. I had a diary at home when I was younger, but lost it when I was deported.

However, during my time in the slave-labour factory, I managed to 'organise' (this means steal!) a few leaflets which were blank on one side. I also found a piece of string and a stub of a pencil. I made a book out of the leaflets and string and wrote down all the poems I used to love, and conversations I had with people. On arrival in Auschwitz, the Nazis had taken everything away from us, but they could not take away our memories and thoughts.

Sadly, I lost this little book on the last day of the death-march. I was very upset when I realised it had gone, because it was really my talisman. I felt that as long as I had this book, my only tie with the past, I would stay alive.

## Was it possible to establish friendships while in the camp? (18-year-old, Germany)

Yes, it was certainly possible. Not everyone thought only of themselves. Many of us had things in common from our pasts in Hungary. And we were hungry and cold together, which brought us closer. The group I was in did not move around very often and it was not split up, so we did develop lasting friendships.

## Did news of the escape at Sobibor spread to your camp and give hope to your fellow prisoners? (13-year-old, England)

No, we did not hear about Sobibor at the time. Although all 600 people there managed to escape, many were shot or blown up in the minefields around the camp. Only about 300 people survived. The nastiest part of the story is that later, after the war, the initiator of the escape went home to Poland and was shot by some Poles, along with other returning Jews. Although the Poles had also suffered under the Germans, many of them had no sympathy for the Jews.

## Did you ever think of escaping? (14-year-old, England)

No. There was just no opportunity to do so. And it might have endangered the lives of others if I had tried.

*Did suicide come as an option? I personally think I would have considered it many times. (14-year-old, England)*

No, I never thought of suicide. I don't remember if I knew at the time, but the guards killed 100 living inmates as a punishment for one person committing suicide. You were not even allowed to cause your own death – they wanted to kill you. If I did know this at the time, it would certainly have prevented me from killing myself. I would not have wanted to be responsible for causing so many deaths, however desperate I was to escape.

More importantly, I was 20 years old and I did not want to die yet. Instead, I was determined to fight. The Germans wanted us exterminated, but I didn't want to give them the satisfaction of another dead Jew.

*Why were 100 people killed when one person committed suicide? (16-year-old, Germany)*

Those who were not gassed on arrival in Auschwitz were forced to work in factories until they died of exhaustion. The Nazis did not like it if one of the slave-workers opted out and chose to kill themselves. Only the Nazis had the power of life and death.

Killing so many inmates was not a very logical response on their part, as they lost 100 potential slave-labourers. But those were the orders, and orders had to be carried out – even if they were against common sense. Those in command are not always the wisest of men. Anyway, there were always enough prisoners to replace the ones killed.

There was probably another reason as well. The only way to commit suicide in Auschwitz was to throw yourself onto the high-voltage electric fencing which surrounded the camps. When this happened, the body stuck to the wire. The electricity had to be switched off and the fence cleaned, which was hard work and not very pleasant. And while the electricity was switched off, the camp was much less secure. So the Nazis hated it when this happened and did their best to prevent it.

*Were you punished for being involved with sabotage work? (14-year-old, Germany)*

If I had been caught, I would definitely have been tortured to make me reveal the other members of the group. I would most probably have been killed afterwards – shot, hung, or tortured to death. Luckily I was never found out. I would certainly not be alive to tell my story if I had been.

## Did any of the guards ever hurt you physically? (14-year-old, England)

Once, when walking barefoot on very sharp stones, I tripped and stepped out of line. The next second, I received such a strong blow on the back of my neck that I fell to the ground and was very dizzy. Despite this, I had to get up immediately and keep on walking, otherwise I would have been shot.

One of our commandants in Hessisch-Lichtenau was an outright sadist and never went anywhere without his whip. He would have hit me if I had gone near him; he hit anyone in his vicinity, but I was always very careful to avoid being near him.

## Did you have any really valuable possessions taken away from you? (14-year-old, England)

My family lost many possessions. My grandmother came from a famous jeweller's family who had been suppliers to the King and the Kaiser during the Habsburg Empire until the end of World War I. Both she and my mother had many valuable jewels.

When the Germans annexed Austria, my grandmother sent her jewels from Vienna for safe keeping to one of my father's Austrian patients on the Hungarian border. We used to go into the mountains for hikes and managed to take them back home, carrying them and many other valuables in our backpacks. We brought over a precious hand-painted dinner-set for 48 people, with matching silver cutlery. In the forest we picnicked on Persian carpets with silver cutlery, which was not exactly our usual practice when hiking!

We also had valuable musical instruments and antique furniture in our home, as well as beautiful and expensive silver and porcelain objects. Naturally it was all lost when we were deported.

## Do you have any photos of your family left? (14-year-old, England)

Yes, I am very lucky, I do have quite a number of photos of my family. As a girl I had a wonderful wall-unit made for me by a joiner who was one of my father's patients. That kind of furniture was very modern in those days. A Christian friend who always admired it took it to the town where she lived and looked after it. After the war she offered my brother food in exchange for the wall-unit, since she was so fond of it. But she gave him all the photo albums from the drawers, and my brother sent them to me.

### How did you deal with sexual urges while you were in the camps? (14-year-old, Germany)

I have no idea how it was for other people. For me it was not an issue at all. Even though I was 20 years old and had already been in love, my sexuality was very underdeveloped. Possibly this was a result of starvation and dehydration – the body prioritises survival over anything else. For example, we only menstruated once, right at the beginning of our stay, and never again after that.

### What things did you miss while you were in the camps? (14-year-old, England)

In Auschwitz I missed water to drink and wash with; also food, any food. Later on I began to miss books and music, though one day the camp orchestra came and played Mozart to us.

### How did you feel when you heard music in the camps? Did it happen often? (University student, England)

Music always played an extremely important part in my life, from early childhood on. In Auschwitz-Birkenau we were stripped of our last inch of humanity and cut off from our past, so when I heard the sound of the small orchestra playing Mozart's *Eine kleine Nachtmusik*, it was a reminder of civilisation, of my former life. Everyone ran towards the sound of the music. I began to cry. By that time, 1 August 1944, I had learned to distrust anything that happened in the camp and my first thought was, 'What devilish trick is this? What torture is to follow?'

As we were not assigned work there, this was the first time I realised that people were used as musicians in the orchestra. Incidentally, *Eine kleine Nachtmusik* had more value back then; it was not played several times every day on the radio or used for adverts as it is now. Thinking back, I believe the camp orchestra also played some music by Strauss - Johann not Richard; I seem to remember waltzes, maybe the *Blue Danube*? I don't really remember. In those days I was a musical snob and Strauss was not important, Mozart was.

The orchestra actually brought me back into contact with my cousin. She was quite a gifted pianist but I had lost contact with her during my teens: she was brought up Christian, while I was strongly Jewish. That day, she came to listen to the music as well. Otherwise, we would never have met each other in the camp because she was in another barrack and you could not change barracks. She was very disorientated and held my hand begging me not to leave her. We were separated when we had to go back to our respective barracks and did not see each other again. Luckily, my cousin survived.

In Hessisch-Lichtenau we used to sing songs by Schubert, Brahms and Schumann, and real Hungarian folk-songs, the ones collected by Bartok and Kodaly. Snobbery again! If you liked classical music in those days, you refused to have anything to do with popular tunes. We also sang Hungarian, French and German nursery songs. As I had an immense repertoire and a good, clear, and apparently pleasant, voice I was always asked to sing.

When I was a slave-labourer in Hessisch-Lichtenau, we usually walked to the factory, but sometimes we were taken part of the way in a train in two wagons. There was no light in the station when the train came in and we had to jump on very quickly. One day everyone else happened to go into the other wagon and I thought I was completely alone. I felt free and elated. I hadn't been alone for such a long time! I started to sing the first song that came into my head, the *Lullaby* by Brahms.

Suddenly a male voice asked, 'Who is it singing so beautifully?', and one of our guards came up to me. He asked why I sang so well in German and I told him my mother came from Vienna and I had always spoken German with her. He asked, 'Do you play an instrument?', and I replied that I used to play the cello. He then asked if I ever played the recorder and I told him that I had taught it to young children. 'Would you like to have one?', he asked, and I replied that I would love it. 'My daughter has several recorders. I will ask her to send me one for you,' he promised. I thanked him and then he left. From that day on, when I saw him occasionally in camp, he would say that the recorder was on its way, and once he brought me a bowl of real soup from the guards' mess. But the recorder never arrived.

The man's name was Neumann and I heard that he was known for his kindness. On our last day in Hessisch-Lichtenau, there was a clothing distribution. I never went to these until everyone else had finished because the women usually fought a lot over the clothes. I just picked up whatever was left, since I lacked all vanity and usually looked like a scarecrow. During this distribution there was even more fighting than usual. One of the guards got annoyed and fired a shot into the hall, injuring one woman's arm. That guard was Neumann.

The musical connection also helped one of my camp-mates to find me after the war. About 15 years ago, she was trying to find out what happened to me. She asked a history teacher who had written about our group of 1,000 Hungarian Jewish women, whether he had ever come across someone called Trude who was very involved in music and had been a nursery school teacher.

This teacher, Dieter Vaupel, was already in touch with me. He knew who my friend meant and gave her my contact details. Judith Magyar Isaacson, as she was then called, met me in 1989 at her book launch in Hessisch-Lichtenau, and we have since been in correspondence (see Bibliography for details of her book).

### If you had the chance to become a work-leader again, would you make the same decision? (14-year-old, England)

I was offered the position of work-leader as a bribe. Two of the camp guards did something wrong and I found out about it. They were aware that the commandant knew me and so were afraid I might tell him what they had done. So they offered me the chance to become work-leader, which meant a better chance of staying alive – more food and an easier workload.

However, it would also have meant that I had to spy on other prisoners, denounce them and push them around. I had a choice. I refused. I don't think that I would make a different decision today, as I still believe in decent behaviour towards my fellow human beings.

### Would it have been possible for a work leader to behave in a decent way? (15-year-old, Germany)

I don't think so. Their job was to be nasty and spy on people. If they hadn't done this, they would certainly have been demoted and punished.

## Were you later ashamed of your behaviour when you pushed the old lady out of the way? (14-year-old, Germany)

Yes and no. I am ashamed of behaving in that way. It was the only time it happened because I was normally a decent, caring and polite person, but I acted as though I was possessed. It was totally out of character. But though I am sorry that I harmed the old woman, I do not regret what I did. Apart from anything else, as she was an old lady, I did not change her fate because the old were all exterminated on arrival at the concentration camps. The Hungarian Jews were the last to arrive and the Nazis were keen to exterminate as many people as possible because it was so late in the war, and so only very strong-looking young people were permitted to live. Ninety per cent of the Hungarians arriving in Auschwitz were sent to the gas chambers straight away.

If anything, I did the old lady a favour because in the deportation from my home town, the usual number of people in a truck was 70–90, but there were 120 in ours. She probably suffered less than she would have done if she had stayed in the group of 50 volunteers to go to another camp, as I did. But, of course, I could not know this at the time. It does not excuse my bad behaviour.

Though I don't normally believe in things like that, on that day I must have had something like ESP (extra-sensory perception). It actually happened to me a couple more times during the war. When we arrived in the new camp, after the incident with the old lady, the first person I saw was my father. My main reason for not staying in Budapest, where courageous Christian friends had offered to hide me, was that I wanted to speak to my father again. When I got back home, he had already been taken away and we had no idea if he was still alive. In the new camp, we were together again for a few more days, although in terrible circumstances, before we were separated for ever.

## What did it feel like to be on the death-march? (14-year-old, England)

Terrible. We were already extremely weak when we started the march. Even though it was April, it was very cold for the season and still snowing. I was in a sleeveless flannel shirt and a very threadbare striped jacket and I was barefoot. We received nothing to eat. We walked in a circle for ten days. Anybody who fell down, collapsed or even could not get up in the morning was shot on the spot. There were fewer and fewer of us left, we were getting weaker and weaker and had little hope of surviving. It was made even more difficult knowing that the Germans had lost the war and both the Americans and the Russians were approaching, from the West and the East respectively. We were so near to freedom and it looked as if we would not make it. When you have hardly any hope, it is even more difficult to keep on hoping. I was extremely lucky to survive.

## What was your happiest memory? (14-year-old, England)

The beautiful sunrise over the bridge on the last day of our death-march, just before I collapsed.

## Were any of your friends or family killed? (13-year-old, England)

Most of my friends, my parents, uncles, my grandmothers and other members of my family were murdered. I usually use the word 'exterminated', because Jews and Gypsies were considered subhuman vermin; and vermin has to be exterminated, preferably by gas.

One of my grandmothers was deported from Vienna, first of all to the transit-camp at Theresienstadt in Czechoslovakia, and later to Auschwitz, where she was gassed. My other grandmother stayed in hiding in Budapest but had to go into the ghetto because there was no one to feed her. There was very little food in the ghetto. She just about survived the war, but died a few days later as she was just skin and bones.

My mother was gassed on arrival in Auschwitz. My father was still alive on 2 August 1944, but I have never been able to find any record of his existence afterwards. He was most probably gassed that day. My brother survived and is still alive.

Many of my more distant relatives died in the Holocaust. Some were lucky and managed to emigrate, though it was difficult. One aunt and uncle were 58 years old when Austria was annexed. They managed to escape via Brussels, Marseilles, Lisbon and Mexico, finally settling in New York. They had to rely on charity because all their money and possessions had been confiscated by the Nazis. It took them two years to reach New York and at the age of 60, they had to build up a new life from scratch. Their three sons also escaped; one went to Australia, one to the Philippines and one to Palestine. Only one of the three brothers ever met his mother again.

50

## How did your brother manage to survive? (14-year-old, England)

In Hungary, all the young men were forced to join the army for military service at the age of 18. Jewish men were taken at all ages between 18 and 50. They were not trained in arms but made to work in mines and road-building. At the age of 19, my brother was taken out of the Music Academy in Budapest and put to work in a mine. The Hungarian sergeant in charge there amused himself by throwing stones down on to the 'Jew-boys'. My brother's hand was injured and this put an end to his promising career as a concert pianist.

Later all the Jewish soldiers from his unit were marched out to the Ukraine. It was a very hot summer; they were given little to eat and were very weak, so they abandoned their military gear. By the time they arrived in the Ukraine, it was freezing and they had no warm clothing. Some died of starvation, some froze to death and the rest were used as guinea-pigs and blown up on minefields. Luckily, my brother and a friend managed to escape during the march and made it to Bucharest. Although the Romanians were mostly very anti-Semitic, they hated the Germans even more, so they gave refuge to the few Jews who reached Bucharest, and my brother stayed there for the rest of the war.

Unfortunately, he never quite recovered from being unable to fulfil his potential. He became a music and piano teacher, an outstanding coach for singers and other instrumentalists, and a writer on music. Though he lives in London now, we see very little of each other; sadly we never really got on. However, I have a very close friendship with his daughter and her family.

## What do you know about what happened to your father? (14-year-old, England)

My father was deported with my mother and me to Auschwitz, arriving on 7 July 1944. That was the last time I saw him because men and women were separated on arrival. According to one of the documents I have, my father was still alive in Auschwitz on 2 August 1944, the day I left for Hessisch-Lichtenau, and that is the last record I have been able to find of him. The document says: 'Domiciled in Birkenau'. Some domicile!

Though there is an International Tracing Centre in Germany with an incredible number of documents recording the movement of people during the Holocaust, there seems to be no record of my father. I applied again a few years ago because many more documents came to light after the Soviet Union was opened up. They replied recently saying that nothing more had been found.

### Did you lose a boyfriend in the Holocaust? (14-year-old, England)

No, but I did lose many very close friends. There was one friend who had asked me to marry him the last time I saw him, before he was killed on the Ukrainian minefields. I was very fond of him but did not want to marry him.

Before the Holocaust, I had lots of friends and a normal social life for the time: we used to go for walks together, go out on our bicycles or go swimming. I still have some photos taken in 1940 and 1941, showing me with various groups of friends. But by 1945, I was the only one of these young people still alive (see Figures 4, 5 and 6). That was the fate of a young girl in Hitler's time.

### How did you feel when you found out that your friends and family were being killed? (13-year-old, England)

At the time, I didn't know that the smoke we saw on arrival and the stench we smelled, day and night, in Auschwitz-Birkenau, came from the gas chambers and the burning of bodies. We only found out later during our time in the camps. I was naturally very sad and upset, though in a way I was glad that my mother did not have to go through what I experienced. I only learned after the war that my father had not survived.

The same is true of my friends. I was in a different transport from most of my friends, and I didn't know at the time that hardly any of them had survived. I didn't think they would die since they were young and strong. They must have been treated even worse than we were.

I have very little recollection of how I felt in those days beside the thought that I had to be very careful not to descend to the same level as the perpetrators. The sadness came after we were freed and we learned about everything that had happened to the people we knew, when the loss became a reality.

To some extent my feelings from then on were paralysed; even today I am unable to grieve when someone I love dies. Perhaps I have built up internal defences because it was the only way I could go on living.

FIGURE 4: Trude, aged 17 (far right), enjoying a walk in her home town with a group of friends in 1941. Trude was the only one to survive.

FIGURE 5: Trude (far left), with her friends on a cycling trip in 1941, visiting the beautiful Romanesque church in Ják near her home town. Trude was the only one to survive.

53

FIGURE 6: *Trude with four nice young men at the swimming pool, 1940. Trude was the only one to survive.*

### You tell your story now in a very factual way; did you show your feelings in those days? (15-year-old, Germany)

You are right, I state the facts because the facts speak for themselves. I do not wish to show false sentimentality or emotion. And because I only give the facts, the same schools ask me to go back and tell my story again and again. In those days I certainly had feelings and suffered very much indeed.

### Which part of the story makes you most emotional? (14-year-old, England)

I suppose the fact that we happened to meet my father, having had no news of him for two-and-a-half months, and we then spent two days in the concentration camp and five days in the cattle-truck together.

## What did it feel like while the Holocaust was going on? (13-year-old, England)

It was extremely frightening, and also disillusioning because many people we thought of as friends did nothing to help us. My father was denounced, possibly by our caretaker or our maid, for the 'crime' of listening to the BBC World Service.

It was dreadful to see my parents being taken away, friends collapsing and dying, dreadful to be really hungry and thirsty, not being able to wash, being dehumanised and not being able to do anything to stop it. It is very difficult to describe how it felt, for example, to have to sit in the muck that overflowed all over the cattle-truck, with no air or water. There was just a feeling of complete powerlessness and hopelessness.

## Did you have to suffer a lot? (14-year-old, Germany)

Quite a bit. It is very painful to be constantly thirsty, with no access to water during a blazing hot summer. It is very painful to be constantly hungry; you get stomach pains and become weak. It is very unpleasant to have to walk barefoot over sharp stones and in pine forests and over snow and ice.

It weakens you when the bedbugs are sucking your blood at night and not letting you sleep, when you work extremely hard during the day and have to walk for two hours just to get to work. It is difficult when you are always terrified because you are at the mercy of vicious individuals and don't know if it is your last day on earth. And when you suspect that your parents and friends were killed and you will never see them again, how could you not suffer?

## Were you disgusted with your physical state in the concentration camp? (14-year-old, Germany)

Yes, but it was not just disgust at the fact that we were dirty and stank – it was the total dehumanisation and humiliation of our situation.

*What did you feel when you were taken to the concentration camp? (14-year-old, England)*

My feelings were mixed. I felt anger because of our helplessness; we were being dehumanised and had no way of escaping. Fear, as I never knew what was going to happen to me next. Resolve, to remain alive without compromising my integrity, so as to thwart the Nazis. And finally despair, because I did not know if I was going to die or survive.

*What did you feel towards the future? (13-year-old, England)*

Hopelessness, mostly, but at the same time I kept a little bit of hope, however unrealistic, that I would survive and one day there would be a better world to live in.

*Could you imagine life after the war? Did you ever have visions of the future, maybe in your dreams? (14-year-old, Germany)*

I had no realistic expectation that I would survive the war. We did have visions of the future, though very simple ones: about the food we would eat, about being warm again. I do not remember my dreams, but we did daydream a lot.

*Did you ever wish to be released through death, or did you ever wish for death for your campmates? (14-year-old, Germany)*

I do not really remember, but I don't think I wanted to die; and there was no reason why I should have wished death on other people.

*What was going through your mind all the time? (14-year-old, England)*

I am sorry but I cannot really give you a proper answer. The uppermost thought in my mind was probably that I was hungry and would like some food, and that I would like to come out of everything alive. We lived from day to day, from hour to hour, and could not think much ahead.

*When you escaped death or saw some beauty in nature, were there moments when it could still make you happy, despite the brutality of day-to-day life in camp? (17-year-old, Germany)*

Yes, certainly. When we arrived in the slave-labour camp Hessisch-Lichtenau, the first thing that made me happy was the sight of trees and grass. I had missed green things in Auschwitz where there was not a single blade of grass anywhere. And when we went to work, though we were tired and weak, I enjoyed the changing seasons, the leaves, the trees, even the sight of white snow.

Naturally, when I managed to survive a selection, I was happy and amazed to find myself still alive. I also appreciated the humanity shown to me by one of the workers in Hessisch-Lichtenau, and once by a German guard.

*What helped you survive the Holocaust? (13-year-old, England)*

First of all luck. Hungary was only occupied in March 1944, so I did not have to endure as long a time in the camps as people from many other countries. Also, I was 20 years old and physically strong, despite having had a serious operation just after the occupation. So I did have a better chance at the outset than many. Later, I was lucky on a number of occasions.

Also, I think it was important and it helped that I tried to keep my integrity. The only exception was the time when I pushed the old lady out of the way to join a different group. The rest of the time I tried to behave like a decent human being, even though it was not always to my advantage to do so.

*What kept you going in times of need? How did you find the strength to keep on fighting for your freedom? (15-year-old, England)*

What kept us going? We fantasised a lot about food. We tried to remember poems we had learned, books we had read, music and songs. I grew up with Schubert, Brahms and Schumann songs and Hungarian, German and French folk-songs. This kept up a tie to our past. We even laughed sometimes; it helped if you had a sense of humour. I always loved and enjoyed everything in life: flowers, trees, landscapes, walking, reading, music, paintings, old friendships, meeting people, new experiences. I did not want to die.

And I was prepared to fight because I felt my death would be one more triumph for the Nazis. But I only wanted to live if I could keep my integrity; staying a decent human being was even more important to me than remaining alive. I would not have wanted to feel guilty for the rest of my life for causing others hardship, or feel ashamed for co-operating with the guards to gain an advantage. I had a choice of how to behave. I repeat – I had to keep my integrity. And that is why I often say that I won the war: the Nazis could dehumanise me physically but not mentally.

### Did you always know you were going to survive? (14-year-old, England)

No, I did not. On the contrary, many times I was certain that I would not make it to the end, but I never totally gave up hope. I was actually very lucky because a number of times I was in a situation where it could have gone one way or the other.

### Can you explain how you escaped death so many times? (15-year-old, England)

No, I cannot. I seem to have been extremely fortunate. The fact that I was young, only 20 years old, meant that I was not gassed immediately. On the other hand, the fact that I had just had a serious operation did not help, and my sabotage activities were not conducive to staying alive. Indeed, being in the sabotage group put me in mortal danger.

I suppose burying the commandant's dog was a piece of luck, since later the commandant removed me from a selection. It was luck too when I was not shot at the end of the death-march. I must have nine lives, for since the war there have also been a number of times when I should not have survived.

### What happened to you after you escaped from the death-march? (14-year-old, England)

After being left on the side of the road, I lay there for some time, but it was still cold. I noticed a wooden, shack-like building nearby. With great difficulty, I managed to drag myself there on my stomach, for I was too weak to stand up or even to crawl. It was a stable full of horses and pleasantly warm inside.

A young German girl came in to feed the horses and when she saw me, she told me it was not safe to stay there because the horses belonged to German soldiers who were outside. She pointed me towards a barn where I would be safe and gave me a piece of bread to eat.

## How did it feel to be liberated? Were you scared? (13-year-old, England)

I do not really remember, but am pretty sure that I was not scared at the time. I was so weak it had not really sunk in that I was free. At the time I was not certain if it was really the end, and I didn't know what would happen to me afterwards. Also, given my physical state, it was touch and go if I would survive. So my feelings must have been rather mixed. But I probably did feel exhilarated, especially when the German girl gave me bread.

## How did you get to England and when did you go there? (14-year-old, Germany)

I decided not to go back to Hungary because Hungary had allowed the Jews to be deported and had even aided the Germans. There was nothing really for me to go back to. My family and most of my friends had been killed. As a result, I lost my Hungarian citizenship and was stateless for many years, which had enormous consequences. I lived first in France, then in South Africa, then in Israel and again in South Africa, not because I liked travelling, but because it was difficult to find a country that would take me.

Finally in 1957, nine years after I first arrived in South Africa, I became a South African citizen. My passport arrived three weeks later, and four days after that my first husband, my eight-year-old son and I were on a boat to England. South Africa was still a Commonwealth country then and after a year in London, I became a British citizen in 1958.

I have lived in London for the past 43 years. I was liberated from the Germans on my twenty-first birthday and it took me another 13 years to become British. Only then was I allowed to cast my vote and exercise my democratic rights for the first time. At last I had all the civil rights that

DID YOU EVER MEET HITLER, MISS?

every citizen is entitled to. This was very important to me.

I can never understand people who say, 'I can't be bothered to vote', and then criticise everything about their country. Many people say, 'It makes no difference whether I vote or not, a single vote will change nothing.' This is wrong – everyone's opinion counts. We can only change the world for the better if we choose to participate in its decision-making processes.

This is one way we can help prevent the injustices of the past from happening again – not just what happened to us during the Holocaust, but also what was done in Germany. So many Germans died unnecessarily as soldiers during the war, or were killed because they were disabled or had genes which Hitler thought were not useful for his master-race. It is very important to make the effort to vote, and not to stand back and wash your hands of responsibility.


## What work did you do after the war? (16-year-old, Germany)

I did a great number of things. For a very long time I did anything I could to put a roof over my head and bread in my mouth. I wrote addresses on envelopes, sang in synagogues, even though I found it hypocritical to sing words I could not believe in, and worked as a weaver and as a Hebrew teacher. It was all very badly paid as I had no work permit and had to work illegally. Once I had a passport and had settled in Britain, I worked as a librarian and eventually finished my working life as a fully qualified university librarian. I have even been given an honorary doctorate in genocide education, despite having left school at 15 with no qualifications!


## Did you ever pose as an Aryan to avoid being captured? (14-year-old, England)

Not during the war. But in 1948 I had to travel through Egypt without a passport or visa. The Jewish authorities advised me to lie and say that I was Aryan, so as not to be locked up and detained in Egypt. For the first time in my life, I denied that I was Jewish, but that was just for one day.

In March 1948, I was travelling by boat from Paris to Durban, in South Africa. On the second day of the journey, we stopped in Naples and I joined an Italian group going on shore. My timetable said the boat would leave at midnight. We had a lovely day. One man and I somehow lost the other Italians in the group and our money ran out. I didn't even have a

60

watch on, all I had with me was a camera.

At 7 p.m. we went back to the boat, intending to have dinner there and go back on shore once more before leaving. To our surprise, the boat had left one hour earlier and we were stranded in Naples: no money, no passport, no visa except a piece of paper given to us when we got off the boat earlier!

My companion was a draftsman who had been in the army in Kenya during the war, and was now going back there to work. The next day we went to his office in Rome and managed to organise plane tickets to rejoin the boat in Suez. The one thing we still needed was a visa for Egypt. I got in touch with the American Joint Distribution Committee in Rome (I had been working in the Paris office before I left) and they told me that under no circumstances must I tell the Egyptian authorities that I was Jewish. There was unrest in Palestine; it was shortly before the State of Israel was proclaimed. If I presented myself as a Jew with no papers or identification, the Egyptians might lock me up.

The Egyptian Consul in Rome was charming. I really don't know how it came about, but I remember distinctly singing him some naughty student songs. He phoned the police in Cairo to tell them to take me off the plane on arrival and onto the ship in Port Said, along with my Italian friend. He did not ask my religion, but the police in Cairo did, and as I hadn't the slightest wish to be locked up again, I did deny being Jewish. It took five days for us to rejoin our ship in Suez. We were lucky though because the voyage through the Suez Canal had been horrendous and everybody was seasick. I on the other hand had had quite an adventure!

### Did you ever consider going to Israel? (15-year-old, England)

Before the war I was a Zionist (someone who believes that the Jews should have their own state) and wanted to live on a kibbutz in Israel. However, after living in close quarters with other Jews in the camps during the Holocaust, I became convinced that I was not suited to communal living. I was too much of an individualist.

When I finally went to Israel in 1949–51, I loved it (even though I had an extremely difficult time) and for the first time in my life, I felt at home. It was the one country where no one asked why I did not go to synagogue! I felt free. I had to leave Israel for family reasons, but I thought it would only be for a few months and intended to return to Jerusalem as soon as possible.

Then things worked out differently and I could not go back. I was homesick for 18 years until I finally returned on a visit. Then I felt it was too late for me to change residence once again. And I was happily married, with an interesting job and a nice home. So we remained in London.

*You mentioned that you had amnesia after the liberation. Could you expand on this? How long did it last? Was it total or partial? What provoked the return of your memory? (University student, England)*

I knew that I didn't want to return to Hungary, but I didn't know what was going to happen to me. I didn't remember anybody's names. I was in Paris for three days after my liberation and could not remember my French godfather's name, or even that I had one, although I used to love him. But then I was put into prison (have you read my book *A Cat Called Adolf*?) because of a nasty individual and, though it eventually turned out to be a mistake, it was four and a half months before I managed to get out. Not a very pleasant thing to happen after having been deported, but they did apologise. When I was put into prison, I was first handcuffed and then put into a small, dirty room with a chair. This whole affair gave me such a shock that I tried to cut my vein on my wrist with a thick piece of glass I found on the floor of the cell. It was the only time I really felt like giving up. However, it jolted my memory. Then luckily I remembered names of people who could prove who I was, but it still took all that time to get out of prison where I found myself with German Nazi women, and French and Italian Fascists. The amnesia lasted some five weeks.

*Did you ever get any compensation from the French authorities for mistakenly locking you up as a Nazi, and were you ever rewarded for the sabotage work you did in the slave-labour camp? (14-year-old, England)*

The answer is no in both cases. When the French authorities released me after four and a half months in prison, I was so pleased that I never thought of suing them. They apologised at the time, but that was all. By the time I thought of it, I found that they had destroyed all the documents relating to my imprisonment, and I could not remember the names of any witnesses.

I have never been given an award for my sabotage work, but we are still fighting for financial compensation for the slave-labour we did in the factories, which of course was not paid. But my reward came when a teacher told me, after hearing about my sabotage group, that she now understood a story her father, a British soldier, had told her. In a battle with the Germans towards the end of the war, he was amazed when they heard the noises of German artillery being fired, but no explosions followed. Those Germans must have been given sabotaged ammunition. That made me really happy.

## Have you ever been attacked for being Jewish since the Holocaust? (18-year-old, Germany)

I have not been mistreated, but I have had a few unjustified anti-Semitic or xenophobic remarks thrown at me – it is difficult to know which of the two they were.

## Were your two husbands also in concentration camps during the Holocaust? (16-year-old, Germany)

No. My first husband, whom I married in Paris in 1946, was Hungarian. After he finished his schooling in Hungary, he went to Belgium to continue his studies of the violin. When Belgium was occupied by the Germans in 1940, he fled to France. He looked like a native Hungarian even though he was Jewish, and he had a fake passport which said he was Protestant, so he was able to get by and escape persecution. But from the end of 1943 onwards, it was still dangerous for him, so he went into hiding in Southern France until the end of the war.

My second husband, Franz, grew up in Berlin. His father owned a factory which he lost in the Wall Street Crash of 1929, so his family were poor. But since Franz was bright, at the age of ten, he won a scholarship to a very good school. When Hitler came to power in 1933, he was 13. The other boys at school beat him up so badly – he was the only Jewish child in his class, and a small and skinny boy – that he was in a coma for three days. Then his scholarship was withdrawn because he was Jewish and he had to leave school. His parents were making handbags and he had to work delivering them to help support the family. Later, he managed to get into a Jewish evening school to continue his studies.

He joined a Zionist group and at the age of 16 went to Palestine where he lived in a youth village. It had a very good school and the youngsters learned a trade while studying, or else worked on the land, as the school was self-supporting. Later he joined the British Army and served for six years, first in the Royal Engineers and then in the Intelligence Services, tracking down and interrogating Nazis in Austria.

### Was your second husband Jewish? (14-year-old, England)

Yes, but he could have been any other religion or none: I would still have married him. Our way of thinking was much on the same lines and we had very similar tastes in most things. Obviously, as a Jew who had also suffered and lost his parents during the Holocaust, he could understand my background much better than someone not affected. But the fact that he was Jewish was not important to me. We did not have a religious wedding.

I have no objection to people of different religions getting married. Of course, there can be drawbacks as it is always difficult for two people to live together, and different backgrounds can make it even more complicated. But then for a religious Jew and an atheist Jew, it would be just as difficult.

### Do you have any children? (18-year-old, Germany)

Sadly, no longer. I had a wonderful, extremely gifted son who had two children of his own. The first was with an English girl when he was much too young to be a father, and so I have a grandson who is now 30. Later, my son married a Frenchwoman and they had a daughter, who is now 24 and has just had a son herself, which makes me a great-grandmother!

My son became professor of genetics at the University of Zürich at the age of 26, at least ten years younger than the usual age for such a position. He also spoke ten languages. Sadly, at the age of 30 he committed suicide. He is one of many children of survivors who did so. What happened to us somehow left its traces in the following generation. This is a recognised fact today.

### Do you know any other survivors and have they coped as well as you have? (14-year-old, England)

Yes, I know quite a number of people who were with me or in other camps, or hiding in terrible circumstances. There is a Holocaust Survivors' Centre in London. There is also a wonderful Holocaust Memorial Centre called Beth Shalom (meaning 'House of Peace') in Nottinghamshire, founded and run by a Christian family, where I meet other survivors. When I go to Hungary, I meet women who were with me at the time and were just as lucky to escape as I was.

Some survivors managed like myself because they were young. Some survived because they were willing to do anything to survive, because they were selfish and aggressive, and in that case they often still are. Some were just lucky. Many are not so fortunate now: though they survived, they never recovered from what they went through, and have not managed to cope with life after the Holocaust. It is very sad to see them like this.

I always had many interests and appreciated everything that life gave me. In this way I am very lucky, and it certainly helped me to cope.

## *Do you ever have any reunions with other survivors? (17-year-old, Germany)*

The answer is yes. My husband and I used to spend a couple of weeks nearly every year in Budapest where I keep in touch with three women who were in the same camp as me. Like me, they speak regularly to schools in Hessisch-Lichtenau, the place where we were made to work in the munitions factory. One woman organises a survivors' meeting nearly every month, and once I was able to attend.

We are all old women now and some of the Hungarian survivors are in dire need because their pensions have not been raised since the Communist regime was disbanded and goods stopped being subsidised. Often they have to decide between buying food, heating their houses or buying the medicine they need, which is very sad. Some of the more educated women managed to build up an income and are not so badly off, but most have to struggle. This is one of the after-effects of the Holocaust, because it disrupted so many people's lives and interrupted their education, preventing them developing their lives as they would otherwise have done. After more than 50 years, some people have started to receive compensation for work in the slave-labour camp, but not all have been given it as yet.

## *I was wondering if you had been back to where you were born? (14-year-old, England)*

I have now been back to Hungary a few times, but it took me many years. The first time, in 1970, it was just for a few hours to see two 80-year-old people who had managed to survive, whom I felt I wanted to see once more. It was lovely to see them, but I hated being in the town, because of my memories of the anti-Semitism I suffered there.

Many years later, in 1992, I was invited to the fiftieth anniversary of our school graduation. I did not actually finish high school and at first did not want to go to the reunion, but some old school-friends I hadn't seen for 53 years asked me so kindly that I changed my mind. There was anti-Semitism in my school but not from the pupils – I do not remember one incident where the pupils were anti-Semitic. And the anti-Semitic teachers were long dead when I went back there. It was a very emotional occasion, and since then I have been in regular contact with three of my friends from school.

In 1994, I was also invited to the fiftieth anniversary of the deportation of the Hungarian Jews. I told the organisers I would only attend if I could speak to the pupils of my old school. I felt strongly that the young people of the town should know what happened there. The headmaster replied by return mail saying he would be honoured if I came to his school to tell my story, and asked permission for another school to attend as well.

After my talk there were lots of questions. One boy obviously wanted to be awkward. He asked, 'Why didn't you emigrate?' I said, 'There is anti-Semitism in other countries as well, we could no longer get in anywhere.' He continued, 'Where do you think there is more anti-Semitism, in America or the Soviet Union?' I replied, 'I don't know, but Russia is certainly more openly anti-Semitic than the US.' 'How can you say this, when the Soviet Union even created a state for the Jews?' he countered.

I was lucky. A name that I had not heard for at least four decades suddenly sprang to my mind. 'You mean Birobidzhan, don't you?' 'Yes,' he said. 'Have you ever looked at the map? Do you know where Birobidzhan is?' He said no. 'Well, it is in the very worst part of Siberia. The very few people who got there hardly managed to survive, it is so desolate; practically nothing will grow there.' The boy stopped asking questions.

### Have you been back to Auschwitz, or any of the other places you were held? (Adult, England)

I went back to Auschwitz recently, even though I did not feel like going there. I am always amazed at people wanting to go to Auschwitz just for one day, and don't agree with the person who organises one-day tours of the camp. However, I might be wrong and some people do seem to have found it instructive.

My feelings at Auschwitz were quite ambivalent. I was very impressed by the bleakness of the museum, but when we went to Auschwitz-Birkenau, the part I was in, which I was most worried about visiting, it meant very little to me. The wooden barracks have disappeared, so has the chimney, and obviously the smoke and the stench have gone. The greyish-yellowish barren soil is now covered with beautifully manicured grass and lovely trees.

I have visited my other main camp in Hessisch-Lichtenau a number of times. I still go there quite often to speak in schools, memorial places and other forums. There used to be a very active Historical Research Group there, consisting mainly of teachers and historians researching the area's history during World War II.

### Did you find it hard to go on after the end of the war? (14-year-old, England)

Yes, it took me a very long time to get back to normal. I was physically weak, ill and traumatised, and my memory was partially gone. Because I did not go back to Hungary, I became stateless, an asylum-seeker. I was permitted to stay in some countries but not allowed to work and earn my living.

When you are stateless, you are an outcast, a pariah. You do not belong anywhere and nobody quite wants you. You have no rights, and because you have no work permit you cannot earn your living, even if you are allowed to take refuge somewhere. So you work illegally in order to eat and put a roof over your head. It is the same today for immigrants and asylum-seekers in this country and elsewhere.

I worked illegally because I was hungry and cold, but if you do not have a work permit, you are always exploited and paid much less than others. I worked very long hours, cleaning other people's homes or writing addresses on envelopes, and still could not earn enough to pay for a room and food as well. Nor was I ever very good at accepting charity. So

I was constantly very hungry and cold, and always aware that the authorities might catch me working illegally. It was lonely, too, because most of my friends had been killed.

I married someone with whom I had very little in common and would certainly not have married under normal circumstances. He was ill and I had to support him, and so was even hungrier. It was a great struggle.

### Were there any lasting physical effects? (14-year-old, Germany)

During my time in camp I often had dysentery, i.e. very bad diarrhoea. Apart from that, I seemed to have quite a strong constitution. Afterwards, however, as a result of being ill-treated – being starved, my menstruation having stopped, and so on – I developed a number of fairly severe health problems.

Immediately after liberation, I suffered from something which in French is called *anémie graisseuse* – in English it translates literally as 'fatty anaemia'. This caused me to balloon from 38 kilograms to 98 kilograms within a few weeks. It attacked my heart and I had to be treated with injections three times a week for six months. I have only found out recently that anaemia was one of the side-effects caused by working with the poisonous substances used as explosives in the munitions factory.

My teeth fell out as a result of malnutrition. I developed very bad osteoporosis and had many broken bones; I only had to bend down over the arm of an armchair to pick something up and I would fracture three ribs! I only had to stub my toe lightly on something and it would be broken.

My spine is in a very sorry state; according to the last scan I had, there is not one vertebra or disc which is undamaged. This cannot be corrected and is painful because as a result I have trapped nerves. But I live with it and am too busy to think of it too much or feel sorry for myself. I only take medication when it becomes really unbearable. But thanks to excellent medical treatment, some of it has at least been prevented from deteriorating still further.

And because I was extremely poor and hungry for so many years after the war, I lived in very damp rooms and developed bad arthritis. Any movement I make is painful. But again I live with it and do not allow myself to take much notice of it, unless a new pain appears which I have to get used to!

## Do you ever have nightmares about your past? (14-year-old, England)

I had very bad nightmares for many years after the war. My doctor had to prescribe tranquillisers and sleeping pills for me because I could not sleep – I suppose I was too frightened to sleep because of the nightmares. After many years, things got better and I was able to cope without medication and only had nightmares occasionally.

Nowadays, I have a few more nightmares again, probably because I speak so much about what happened to me, but now I can cope with them and do not have to take pills.

## Are there any sights, sounds or smells which trigger memories of the Holocaust? (13-year-old, England)

I cannot sit on a sandy beach because it reminds me of the porous earth I had to sit and sleep on in Auschwitz-Birkenau. I cannot go to a public swimming pool, because the sight of women taking showers, naked together, brings back memories. There are other things as well, but these are the worst.

## How did the Holocaust affect your personality? Did you change a lot during the Holocaust? (14-year-old, England)

If I hadn't suffered persecution when I was young, I would not have had to be so aware of what was happening around me. Thus, I was forced to grow up more quickly. I don't think that the events basically changed my character. However, one thing that did affect me was that many people we thought of as friends let us down when it came to the crunch. I learned to trust people less than before, and today I really have to force myself to trust people. I find this very sad because trust is a very important element in human relations. I also used to have very high principles, but nowadays I am a bit more willing to compromise, if somewhat reluctantly.

It affected my family life. My son, a brilliant scientist with a great future, committed suicide when he was 30 years old. Many children of Holocaust survivors did so. These children had no families, no countries, and no roots.

I never take things quite for granted. Somehow my experiences are always in the back of my mind: could it happen again? I always appreciated the good things in life, but since the war I appreciate them even more: the fact that I can have a bath or shower whenever I wish to, that I can eat and do not have to be hungry or cold. I get very upset if anyone leaves food on their plate and it has to be thrown away. Every leftover must be used up, and certainly no bread can be thrown away in my house.

Still, I am happy and as settled as possible. I appreciate decent human behaviour. I always did, but since the war I do so even more. I enjoy every little thing in life: friendship, music, a good book, a beautiful picture, a tree, a flower, a mountain, a meadow. I appreciate being alive and savour all it offers me.

I get very angry with anyone who hurts people, either with words or physically, because of their religion or colour of their skin, or disability. It is sometimes rather tiring, constantly travelling to tell my story at the age of 78, and perhaps if I had not gone through what I did, I would use my retirement differently and allow myself more time to read and make music. But I feel more and more that as an eyewitness, and because we survivors are getting so old and dying out, it is my duty to bear witness to what happened.

### What did being Jewish mean to you during the Holocaust? Has it affected your faith today? (Adult, England)

I certainly had doubts about God before the Holocaust. I have none now; I do not believe in God at all. If there was a God, then the Holocaust and all the other terrible things in the world would not have been permitted to happen; hence I cannot believe that there is a God. If the one and a half million children who were exterminated in camps had to pay for 'the sins of the fathers up to the third and fourth generations', what terrible crime must we and our forebears have committed?

I am afraid I never understood how people could remain religious in camp. There were people who never lost their faith, which in a way I admire. I also know people from very religious backgrounds who lost their faith and then after a while went back to religion, and I cannot understand this. But everyone has to live according to his or her own beliefs and as long as they show tolerance towards others, I have no right to interfere.

To come back to the question of how it affected my faith more precisely, the only thing that has remained constant in my life is being Jewish. I was born Hungarian, my mother was Austrian, and after the war I lived in France, South Africa, Israel and finally in England. The only fact in my life that never changed was that I was Jewish. It is very difficult for me to explain what that means to me. According to some fundamentalists, I would not be Jewish at all, as I am not traditional in my observances. According to Jewish law, I certainly am because my mother was Jewish.

In England, except for a few months, I always worked at Jewish institutes. My last job was as librarian of all the Jewish material, two libraries and two archives, at University College, London. And I am still involved with Jewish matters.

My only identity is being Jewish. Yet it has nothing to do with religion; I do not believe in the Jews as a race. And as I live in England, I am not a Jewish nationalist, though I love Israel and believe that it has the right to exist. I am not proud of being Jewish, because as far as I am concerned, one can only be proud of something that one has achieved, not an accident of birth. But nor was I ever ashamed of being Jewish. I found that quite a few religious people in Hungary were and still are.

My own belief is in the following. Let me tell you a story. There were two Jewish sages, one called Shamai and one called Hillel. A heathen once came to Shamai and asked him to teach him the Torah (the Jewish law, written in the Five Books of Moses) while he was standing on one leg. Shamai was not a very patient old man; he got angry and said to the heathen, 'I have studied the Torah my entire life and am still studying it, and you want me to teach you the whole thing while you stand on one leg! Get out of here!'

The heathen then went to Hillel and repeated his request to him. Hillel said, 'It is simple. Do not do unto others what you would not have done to yourself,' and then he stopped.

The heathen said, 'Carry on.' Hillel replied, 'That is everything, all the rest is just comment.'

This is what I believe in and this is how I have always tried to live.

### Did you ever wish you were not Jewish? (14-year-old, Germany)

I don't think so. I certainly cannot remember ever having done so. I was born Jewish and though I am not at all religious, being Jewish is part of my personal identity. I have the right to be Jewish and I believe I have the right to be accepted as such; and if I deserve respect, to be respected as a Jew as well.

*Was it hard to come to terms with the Holocaust once it had ended? (14-year-old, England)*

It is still hard to come to terms with it. The Nazis killed my parents and most of my friends; the Holocaust ruined my youth. I became an asylum-seeker, wandered from country to country, often worked illegally, and was frequently hungry and cold. Basically, I never quite came to terms with it.

*How did you set about rebuilding your life? (17-year-old, England)*

After liberation, it was difficult to prove that I had been a concentration camp inmate. I had no tattoo on my arm, no documents at all, and I had always kept my red cheeks. The few people who listened to my story said, 'You are young and free, just forget it all and start again.' This was rather difficult; what I had experienced was not something that is easily forgotten.

But I was young and I did manage to pull myself together; finally it was a revenge on the Germans. They had wanted me to die, and I was alive and could rebuild my life. I felt that I had won. They could only dehumanise me physically, but not mentally and certainly not morally, because I had tried to behave in a way that enabled me to retain my integrity. I had a choice, which gave me strength.

*Have you been able to put the past behind you and start again? (14-year-old, England)*

Yes and no. As I cannot and do not wish to forget, I have not put the past behind me. For many years, it affected my everyday life. I had problems sleeping, would scream in my sleep, and had anxiety attacks even in the daytime. I was often hungry. I could not trust people, then for the wrong reasons I trusted the wrong people. I did not have many qualifications as I missed out on education because of the circumstances, and the few I had were not recognised, so it was hard going. In the end I won, and to a certain extent I did manage to overcome the experience and build a new life. But it took nearly a lifetime.

If I had put it all behind me, I would not go out and speak about it. However, that does not mean that my life has been nothing but thinking about the Holocaust. I have lived my life working, looking after my family, having friends, enjoying holidays, reading books and writing about other things as well.

### Do you think you could ever forgive the people who did this to you? (14-year-old, Germany)

No, nor do I wish to. I cannot forgive on behalf of those who were killed, and I do not wish to forgive what happened to me. I certainly cannot forgive Hitler and those Germans who did dreadful things such as killing, torturing, maiming and experimenting on people. Medical people take an oath that their duty is to heal patients, which does not mean carrying out 'scientific' experiments on human beings.

But that does not mean that I hate all Germans, or for that matter all Austrians, Poles, Hungarians or people from other countries that participated in or permitted the Holocaust to happen (which would even include some people in the UK). I certainly do not wish to have any enmity with the people who behaved decently and courageously, or were too young to understand at the time, or were not born then, that is, the second and third generations.

### I was amazed to hear you say that you had no bitterness against your enemies and had forgiven them. I find this truly remarkable as, although I am a Christian, I find it very hard to forgive people on occasion. (University student, England)

It was good of you to write to me, only I am rather sad that I have to disappoint you. There must be some misunderstanding, for I certainly never said that I forgive those who committed the crimes. I do not forgive anyone who harmed me and made such a mess of my life, nor could I forgive on behalf of those who are not alive to forgive for themselves. I have always avoided meeting anyone in Germany of my age or older, for fear that I might have to shake hands with someone who might have killed or tortured my parents or friends, the children I worked with or anyone else.

No, I have not forgiven and cannot do so. I do feel hatred towards the real perpetrators. And as I am still alive and have to bear the consequences of my deportation and internment, I do not see why war criminals who committed atrocities should not be brought to court. At least they have the right to a defence for the crimes they committed, which is the way people are treated in a civilised society. We had no defence, we had committed no crimes.

*Do you feel better towards the SS soldiers? (14-year-old, England)*

Certainly not. They behaved in an inhuman way. Many of them have not changed their attitudes today and are leaders of the neo-Nazis, the new version of the Nazi party, in Germany and Austria. They have no regrets about what they did, so why should I feel different towards them?

*What do you think, looking back, really motivated the camp guards who were in charge of all the prisoners? (Adult, England)*

If I remember rightly, in Auschwitz the guards were from the SS (*Schutzstaffel*: the part of the German army that ran the concentration and death camps), who believed in all the Nazi doctrines. They were nasty individuals, never showing any sign of humanity. Many of them were not actually German but other nationalities, Ukrainian, Austrian, Latvian, Lithuanian or Polish.

In Hessisch-Lichtenau the guards were from the *Wehrmacht*, that is, the normal German army, but many of them enjoyed showing their power, though some did occasionally display some humanity when it was not dangerous. The women guards were very simple women, civilians, who were suddenly able to lord it over us. Most of them did not even volunteer but had been called up for service. How many people would be able to resist suddenly being given the power of life and death? However, they were part of the SS.

*Did you hate the Germans while you were in the various concentration camps? And did you think all Germans were Nazis? (15-year-old, Germany)*

I did not hate all Germans, only the Nazis who treated us in an inhuman way. In those days I thought that it was only the SS who committed the atrocities. Although most of our male guards in Hessisch-Lichtenau were ordinary German soldiers, some of them were more decent than others. I was sure then that not all Germans were Nazis.

Sadly, in recent years it has become clear that German civilians did co-operate with the Nazis much more than was originally thought. At first, when soldiers were ordered to shoot old people, women and children into mass graves, their commanders told them they could opt out if they wanted to; there would be no punishment. (As far as I know, there was only one exception, when the commandant once killed a soldier who refused to obey the order to shoot.) Those who took up the offer were transferred to another unit, but there was no stigma attached. Sometimes they were transferred to the front, but not always. Yet only very few chose to leave the camps.

Of course, it is less dangerous to shoot unarmed people than to fight in the front line and possibly be killed by the enemy. But sometimes they even brought their wives and girlfriends along to take photographs showing how brave they were!

### Did you ever have thoughts or plans for revenge for what the Nazis were doing to you? (14-year-old, Germany)

At the beginning I certainly had thoughts of revenge, but never actual plans. If I had made plans for revenge, then I would have descended to the moral level of Hitler and the people who helped him.

### I hope the people who ill-treated you or murdered people were adequately punished? (14-year-old, Germany)

As far as I know, very few of them were punished. Many were tried after the war, but most of them were set free. For many years afterwards, most of the professions in Germany were still occupied by people who had participated in the Nazi regime. Only people who had joined the Nazi party were allowed to be judges during the Nazi period. After the war, therefore, it was not possible to find untainted judges, unless the odd emigrant returned to office. Often, the perpetrators were set free because the judges were afraid their own misdeeds would be made public as well. They protected the criminals in order to protect themselves. I would have liked to see people judged by younger lawyers who were not part of the old Nazi system, and could have been much more impartial.

Other war criminals managed to flee abroad and escape justice that way. Foreign countries, including the UK, often blackmailed them into becoming spies, in return for a place to settle. They were used during the Cold War because they were often fluent in the languages spoken in countries behind the Iron Curtain. The Vatican is known to have issued visas to former Nazis, which enabled them to escape.

After the war I lived in South Africa for a while. A friend of mine ran a guest farm with her husband in the hills of Natal and invited me to spend a few days there. We had a lot of time to talk and I told them my story. One evening during dinner there was a violent tropical storm. A car stopped in front of the house, and out came a couple with two or three children. They were brought into the dining room to be served dinner. As one naturally does when new people come in, I looked in the direction of the newcomers. Then something clicked and I looked back again and started to tremble.

My hosts noticed and asked what was wrong. I told them that the man had been my camp commandant in Hessisch-Lichtenau. Willi Schaefer was sitting in the same room as me. My host got up, went over to the new guests' table and spoke to them. They left the room. My friend told me that he had persuaded them to have dinner in their own room, and he had asked them to leave before 6 a.m. the next morning so as not to meet any of the other guests.

Later, people often asked me why I did not denounce the man there and then. There were several reasons. One was that South Africa harboured many former Nazis, and nobody would have cared anyway. Another reason was that Schaefer had saved my life at one point because he took me out of a selection to Auschwitz, where I would otherwise have been exterminated. Perhaps I could not hate him because of this. He was never a sadist, though he did some bad things because of following orders indiscriminately. Later I heard that the German authorities were looking for him and he had vanished without a trace.

*How do you feel towards war criminals? Do you think action should be taken now against people who are discovered to have been involved in the Holocaust? (15-year-old, England)*

My answer is definitely yes. Let me explain the reasons why; it is not vengeance but justice that I wish to see.

In a civilised country, if we think someone has committed a crime, we put them before a court which weighs the evidence to decide whether they are guilty or not. If they are guilty, it is just that they are punished, however long ago the crime was committed. This is not revenge, because that would be descending to the mentality of the criminal; it is making sure that justice is done.

War criminals are no different. Some people say that they are too old to be punished, that 50 years have passed since then and we should let bygones be bygones. We survivors are also old, and we and even our children still have to live with the consequences of what these people did to us, of being persecuted and deported. Those who were killed only have the survivors to speak for them. The fact that these criminals escaped punishment and lived all these years in peace does not mean that they should be let off now. A murderer who only murdered one person is punished. Why should one deal differently with a mass murderer?

*How should the law punish genocide, not just the Holocaust but the terrible events in Rwanda and Bosnia? Is it possible ever to punish all those responsible? (Adult, England)*

I am not sure how qualified I am to give you an answer. I certainly know too little about the laws of the countries concerned, or international law. But I will try to tell you what I think.

I agree that genocide, wherever it happens, is terrible and should be stopped. However, the Western economy thrives on arms sales because they create a great deal of employment. Hence, it is not in governments' interest to stop wars, and often economic advantage takes priority over the preservation of human life.

One needs to be careful when using the term 'genocide' because sometimes conflict is more of an internal matter. On occasion, groups within a country attack each other as part of a struggle for power. Sometimes both groups are provided with arms by other countries. It is the only way the arms manufacturers can get rid of obsolete weapons in order to sell new ones. Then the Western countries make a big fuss about morality and the terrible behaviour of the war criminals, who in some cases were even trained by the West. Justice takes a back seat. This thought is not very appetising, but there is very little that can be done about it.

The Holocaust was not caused by arms manufacturers, and the partners involved were certainly not equal. Nor was it an internal affair. Hitler occupied other countries, and at first the Allies let him get away with it. He had an obsession with the Jews, but the Jews were used as scapegoats everywhere over the centuries. In England, there were many who supported Hitler, even though he broke his promises to smaller countries such as Czechoslovakia. Edward VIII, the Cliveden Set and the Astors were all supporters of Hitler.

After the war, war criminals were given refuge in many countries including the UK, because they were useful; for example they could be blackmailed into being spies. People were against prosecution, probably out of fear that they themselves would be exposed and many so-called 'respectable' citizens would be implicated.

I do think that all those who planned genocide, those who gave the orders and those who performed them should stand before a court. Not because we should take revenge on them, but because this is in accordance with the laws of civilised countries. And we must hope that the creation of the International Criminal Court will go some way towards achieving this.

## How do you feel towards the Germans today? (14-year-old, England)

Until 1970 I refused to go to Germany, Austria or Hungary. At the time I thought I would never visit Germany again, but in fact I did go back there for the first time in 1984. My book, *A Cat Called Adolf*, is the result of that journey. I went because my husband started to write on German-Jewish history, and as I worked for many years as a librarian and archivist, I was able to help him in his research. So we went to Germany quite frequently. I have some wonderful German friends who were either young or not born during the war, and I certainly do not hold them responsible for anything. Today there are groups of teachers who speak in schools and try to educate their pupils about what their elders did, explaining why it was wrong. Anyway, I do not believe that one should speak of 'the Germans', 'the Jews', 'the Blacks', but of individual people who make their own moral choices independently.

## Do you still feel hatred when you come to Germany? (18-year-old, Germany)

No. Obviously, I hate the perpetrators – Hitler and other Germans of my generation who participated in the killings and torture. However, even in that period there were people of great courage who tried to help Jews, who hid them away and kept them alive. So I try never to talk about 'the Germans' as a whole. I try not to generalise. There have been two new generations of Germans since the end of the Third Reich, and I certainly do not hate them.

I am often invited to speak in Germany by institutes, church communities and schools. I meet many people who try very hard to make sure that people do not forget what happened there. That is why they invite me and why they also published my book in Germany. I believe it is very important that Germany's younger generation should not be made to feel guilty. Guilt can only lead to hatred.

78

Once, when I told my story to a group of adults in Germany, I noticed that a man in the audience was in tears. At the end of my talk, he told me that he had been a young soldier during the war, two years younger than me, and was captured in his first battle at the age of 18. He was only released from a Russian prison in 1947. When he came back to Germany and learned what had happened in the name of his people, he was ashamed that he had been willing to give his life for a country that could perpetrate such terrible crimes.

### What influenced you to return to Germany to tell your story? (16-year-old, Germany)

It was not an easy decision to make. However, as I was physically able to go, I felt it was my duty to do so. Eyewitness reports make a much bigger impression on people than seeing events on the screen or reading about them. I have a feeling that when I tell my story, the audience knows that I am sincere. Also, they see that though I am Jewish, I am just like them and their grandmothers, and not a devil who wishes to hurt people and must be exterminated.

### Do you find it hard to tell your story here in Germany where it all took place? (16-year-old, Germany)

For many years I had mentally wiped Germany, Austria and Hungary off the map. But I am pleased that since 1984 I have overcome my inhibitions and returned to these places again. There are two new generations who want to know what happened during the war. They are the ones who have to live with the consequences of the actions of their grandparents' generation.

That is why I like getting questions from German students, because it helps me to clarify anything that was misunderstood. And maybe if we work together, these things will not happen again.

### How do the Jewish people in your circle think about Germany now? (18-year-old, Germany)

Many of the other survivors I know say they would never go to Germany and do not understand how I can do it. I try to explain that today's generation is not guilty, and they need to understand what their grandparents' generation did, rather than be punished for it.

## Would you like to live in Germany again? (14-year-old, Germany)

I never lived in Germany. My only long stay in Germany was when I was deported there from Hungary in 1944, when I did not go of my own free will. Nor would I like to live in Germany today. My second husband came from Berlin and had to flee to Palestine at the age of 16 to save his life. Both his parents were killed by the Nazis; his father was a slave-labourer with Siemens, and had to work extremely long hours and walk miles to work because Jews were not allowed to take trams. He was well over 60; it was too much for him and it killed him. His mother was deported and exterminated in Auschwitz. My husband would certainly not have wished to return to Germany for good.

With such memories, most people cannot live in the country which caused them. We often visited Germany together because my husband wrote a history of the Jews and we carried out research in local archives. But we would not have wanted to live there.

## Do you enjoy coming to Germany nowadays? (16-year-old, Germany)

Germany is a beautiful country. I have difficulty meeting people of my age unless I know for sure where they were and what they did during the Nazi period. But most of the people I meet are second or third generation, so they could not have been involved, and I find them friendly, welcoming and helpful.

In the late 1970s, while I was still refusing to go to Germany, my husband and I stayed in Luxembourg, very close to the beautiful old German city of Trier. My husband wanted to visit the city and I reluctantly agreed, but only for one afternoon. When we arrived there, we stopped first at a large square where we saw a stall selling *Bockwurst* – a longer and thicker version of a Frankfurter sausage. My husband bought some. We found that the vendor was Israeli and had a nice conversation with him in Hebrew. Then we proceeded into the town. As both of us had trouble with our feet, our usual first errand was to find a shoe shop. We went to two shops and the staff in both were very helpful and friendly. It made my decision to hate Germans feel very shaky to say the least. After that, we visited the magnificent sights of the medieval city, but we still went back to Luxembourg for the night.

*In your book you describe your first visit to Germany. How did you come to terms with it and what is your attitude to present-day Germany? (18-year-old, Germany)*

Nowadays I work a lot with German teachers or ex-teachers, with other professionals and Christian-Jewish Institutes dedicated to Holocaust education, and I have made friends with many of the second and third generation. I like going to Germany because I see how very many people try to do everything in their power to ensure that what happened should never happen again. I respect them because they are fighting for something they believe in.

In spite of my age (I am 78 years old) and my somewhat defective health, which makes it difficult for me to travel much, I continue to do so for as long as I can because I believe that if a survivor relates his or her experiences, people receive a different message from the one they get from books, films or documentaries, or from hearing about it second-hand. I hope that I encourage those who hear me to think about what happened, and how it can be avoided.

*Do you think it is true, as some historians argue, that ordinary Germans were just as much to blame for what happened in the Holocaust? (Adult, England)*

I am no historian and therefore not qualified to give you an expert's answer, but I shall give you my personal views. I just happened to read a review in the *New York Review of Books* of Daniel Goldhagen's *Hitler's Willing Executioners*, which seems to give an answer to your question. Goldhagen describes how not only the SS but many ordinary Germans, policemen, and so on, participated in and perpetrated Hitler's genocide. It makes very sad reading indeed.

It is hard to understand why so many people followed Hitler and his henchmen. I have often been asked questions about German collective guilt, and have had no real answer until now. I try to emphasise instead that there were some people who did refuse to take part in the shooting and that in general they were not punished. However, Goldhagen's theories sound extremely convincing.

The persecutors set out to reduce us to the level of outcasts. The Nazis intentionally ruptured the relationships between our neighbours and school-friends and ourselves. As the rest of the population accepted the idea that we were not members of the ordinary human race, they acquiesced silently to our degradation and dehumanisation. The Jews became the 'Other', and once this was generally accepted, the Nazis had a free rein. It was a system in which denunciation was rewarded with praise and acceptance. Pupils denounced teachers and vice versa, caretakers their flat-dwellers, children parents, and all this was encouraged.

### *Do you blame Hitler personally for your suffering or just the Nazis in general? (15-year-old, England)*

Most certainly I blame Hitler, as he was the cause of what happened to us. His obsessive hatred caused suffering and death for many millions. He slaughtered Jews, Gypsies, homosexuals, Poles, Russians, slave-labourers, and often even prisoners-of-war who were legally protected by Human Rights conventions. In euthanasia centres like Hadamar, the physically and mentally disabled, German orphans, shell-shocked German soldiers, Germans who were alone and lost after a bombardment, and all who did not agree with him, were put to death.

Naturally he could not do everything on his own, and all those who took part in this incredible destruction of all human values were also to blame.

Hitler was a dictator and had his bullies to carry out his orders. They were strong and people were afraid, but there were occasions when people successfully stood up against them. It is very important to watch out for signs before a dictator manages to obtain so much power; and when people see things happen which they think are wrong, they should stand up against them. It sometimes requires courage, but it is worth it.

### *What kind of a man was Hitler, how did he persuade so many people to join him, and why did he hate the Jews so much? (18-year-old, Germany)*

I am sorry but I do not think I have a good answer. Many people have asked themselves the same questions. It is said that Hitler had enormous personal charisma, and he came along at a time when the Germans needed someone to give them hope. Germany had started World War I and after they lost, the Germans were even more demoralised by the Versailles Treaty. They suffered from terrible inflation and unemployment, and many were homeless and hungry. In these circumstances, anyone offering to make things better would be most welcome.

Then Hitler came along, a man with a great persuasive voice, promising to provide work and food for the Germans, and restore the world's respect for their country. It was true that he did create work for his people, but sadly it was all geared to war. He built factories to make tanks, and roads for the tanks to roll smoothly along. Everything went towards the war effort – and he told the people that this time the Germans would be victorious. So people believed in him and were very grateful.

Before World War II, less than one per cent of the population in Germany was Jewish, and the Jews mainly lived in towns. Most Germans had never met a Jew, so when they were told all kinds of terrible things about them, they did not evaluate Hitler's words or his propaganda machine led by Goebbels and *Der Stürmer*, the most hideous of the national newspapers. They just believed them. This was very dangerous, and many people co-operated in the hope of rising in the Nazi regime and gaining power for themselves. For many it simply came down to ambition.

There are many theories (true or false) as to why Hitler had such an intense personal hatred of Jews, including the following:

- Because he was rejected to study painting at the Academy of Arts in Vienna, and the professor who rejected him was Jewish.
- Because his father, who was born out of wedlock, was fathered by a Jew who did not marry his mother.
- Because he was rejected by a Jewish woman with whom he was in love.

No one really knows the origin of his obsession, or if any of the above was really the cause. All we know is that he certainly had a rather warped mind.


### Did you know Hitler had Jewish blood? I found that hard to believe. (15-year-old, England)

There are rumours that Hitler's father was the illegitimate son of a Jewish father. According to Nazi racial theory, this would have meant that Hitler had Jewish blood. In Judaism, you are only Jewish if your mother is Jewish.

If Hitler believed he had Jewish blood, it would explain a great deal. He would have felt he had to prove that he was a better Christian than anyone else by hating the Jews even more than others, so that nobody would suspect his ancestry. This is also a normal phenomenon among people who change their faith.

### *Do you think that Hitler's suicide was cowardice, because it helped him to escape punishment? (16-year-old, Germany)*

I am not sure – and we will never know – whether escaping punishment was the main reason for his suicide. During one of his last conversations with his favourite minister, the architect Albert Speer, Hitler said that he was disappointed. He wanted to build up a master race, but since the Germans had lost the war, they were obviously not a master race and it therefore did not matter how many Germans died. To me his disappointment, the failure of his big idea, sounds a more likely reason as to why he killed himself. There are other theories, but it is not worth the time and paper to elaborate them.

### *Did you ever see Hitler? What were your feelings towards him at the time? (18-year-old, Germany)*

No, I never saw Hitler in person and I would not have been pleased to meet him. I saw far too much of him in newspapers and photographs as it was. As far as I know, he never visited a concentration or extermination camp. Hitler never wanted actually to see the horrors which he caused. My feelings towards him were hatred, certainly, but also amazement that he could persuade so many people to take part in these inhuman acts.

### *I would like to ask you, if you met Hitler face-to-face today, what would you say? (14-year-old, England)*

My dear, I have no idea. Perhaps I would say, 'What an absolute fool you were,' because in the end Hitler lost and took his own life. He wanted to build up a thousand-year empire with an absolutely pure race, when no such thing exists.

Or I would say, 'What a vile creature you were,' because Hitler used his own people to win his power games. At the end of the war, when he knew the Germans were losing, he did not care how many of his soldiers died. He even sent boys of 15 and 16 out to the front with one day's training, where they were certain to be killed. He believed that since the Germans were losing the war, they had let him down; they were not the very special people he had thought. So it did not matter how many of them died. As the high-ranking Nazi Albert Speer records in his memoirs, Hitler said to him in March 1945,

> If the war is lost, the people will be lost also. It is not necessary to worry about what the German people will need for elemental survival. On the contrary, it is best for us to destroy even these things. For the nation has proved to be the weaker, and the future belongs solely to the stronger eastern nation. In any case only those who are inferior will remain after this struggle, for the good have already been killed.[1]

But probably I would not be able to say anything, and would only have to struggle with myself not to descend to his level and spit in his face or torture or kill him, because he caused so much pain, trouble and human loss.

### *We have been learning about the Holocaust in history and what Hitler did to you Jews is appalling and disgusting. He used you as scapegoats and that's not fair. (14-year-old, England)*

You write 'Hitler used you Jews as scapegoats.' In a way this is true, but it is not the whole story. Hitler did make the Germans believe that the Jews caused all the ills that befell them, which was not at all true. But there was much more to it than that.

For some reason, Hitler had an obsessive hatred of the Jews. Even today there is no clear explanation why. He decided that the Jewish race must be exterminated. There are documents proving that even in the early 1920s, long before the war, the Nazis compiled lists of the Jews in Germany in preparation for their annihilation. Even in February 1945, when the war was nearly over and the Germans had no hope of winning, there were still people occupied in cataloguing and photographing seventeenth- and eighteenth-century cemeteries, hoping that after the war they could find out which Germans had Jewish ancestry in order to get rid of them.

This obsession took priority over the war. In March 1944, it was quite obvious that the Germans were losing. Yet they still chose to occupy one

---

1. Albert Speer, *Inside the Third Reich* (London: Sphere Books Ltd, 1970), p. 588.

of their allies, Hungary. Today there is a theory that the main reason was to ensure that Hungarian Jews were deported before the end of the war. It is hard to understand such an obsession. During wartime a country needs all its manpower and rolling stock. Yet there were soldiers and trains available for the deportation of Hungary's Jews and 430,000 people were taken within seven and a half weeks; all the provinces were 'cleansed' of Jews! It had all been efficiently organised and prepared in advance by Adolf Eichmann.

*Did Hitler really think he could create a superior race of perfect humans, when he was causing such inhuman acts? What shocked me was that he also wanted the liquidation of homosexuals, disabled people, and anyone without blonde hair and blue eyes. (14-year-old, England)*

Hitler believed that Germany should be made into a racially pure nation, not that there is any such thing. People have always intermarried; for example, England was invaded by Vikings, Normans, Romans and, during Roman times, by the Scythians in Lancashire. People from England have intermarried with the Scots, the Welsh, the Irish and with many other nationalities in the colonies, hence there can be very few pure English. All countries have a similarly mixed history.

Besides, it is a proven fact that groups of people who keep to themselves and always intermarry are more prone to genetic defects. Hence it is unwise even to try to keep people racially pure.

Oddly, neither Hitler nor many of those who worked with him closely had the Aryan ideal of blonde hair or blue eyes, so he was not even logical on that point.

*I would like to ask if you think any of the Germans ever regretted hurting any of the Jews? (14-year-old, England)*

In Germany less than one per cent of the population was Jewish. There were very many Germans who never met or even saw a Jew. But most young people were in a movement called the 'Hitler Youth'. They were told that Jews were evil, subhuman vermin. As you know, vermin is something that one exterminates, so it was acceptable to kill Jews.

However, there were some people who later understood the meaning of what they heard and were horrified. A few years ago I met a German lady, of my age, who told me that when she was about nine years old (this was in the early 1930s), she used to play with a group of children who would chase a Jew wearing the typical religious Jewish garb: a long beard, a long black frock-coat, a big round black hat. They used to throw stones at him. She wanted to be the same as the other children. But then one day she realised they were doing a terrible thing and stopped playing with them. Sadly, today she is again part of a neo-Nazi group. Some people never learn.

I am sure there were others who had similar moments of revelation. After the war, some young soldiers felt sorry when they started thinking about what they had done. And there were a few soldiers who opted out at the time and refused to kill innocent people.

*My grandparents do not want to speak about their past. One was a convicted Nazi, the other an Italian soldier who was a prisoner-of-war in Russia. You must think I am nosy for asking you questions, but as they do not talk, I wish to find out what happened. (15-year-old, Germany)*

I would never set anyone against their grandparents. However, it is a pity that yours will not speak about what they did. It is a healthy thing to face up to one's past. If your grandparents did something wrong, they have to live with their consciences; or else they still do not understand the harm that Hitler's time did to Germany.

Millions of Germans died because Hitler invaded other countries in his quest to make Germany the ruler of the world. It is true that he did solve the unemployment problem, but all the work he provided was directed towards the war effort. If people had remembered the terrible consequences of World War I, maybe they would have been more reluctant to start a second one.

The reason I tell my story publicly is that I hope people who hear me or other survivors speaking will learn to consider the consequences of such actions in the future, and perhaps prevent such terrible things from happening again.

*How do you feel about people who try to argue that the Holocaust is just a fabrication? As a survivor does it make you angry? (15-year-old, England)*

Neo-fascists and the far-right today try to deny that the Holocaust took place, in order to attract new converts to the cause. As Deborah Lipstadt writes in her book, *Denying the Holocaust*:

> Since World War II, Nazism in general and the Holocaust in particular had given fascism a bad name. Those who continued to argue after the war that Hitler was a hero and national socialism a viable political system, as these groups tended to do, were looked upon with revulsion. Consequently Holocaust denial became important in the fabric of their ideology. If the public could be convinced that the Holocaust was a myth, then the revival of national socialism could be a feasible option.[2]

Some young people are racist and attracted to far-right parties, but they ask, 'What about the Holocaust?' So these groups have to deny that it happened, so as not to deter people from joining them. It does make me angry but more than that, it makes me sad that people have not learned from what happened. People should learn to respect the way of life of others as long as it does not interfere and harm their own. Tolerance is the word. Other people's culture is just as valid as one's own.

The only thing to do with Holocaust deniers is to ignore them, and not give them the publicity which they seek.

## What were your feelings about the trial of David Irving? (17-year-old, England)

David Irving is an extremely thorough researcher, and very clever in the way he deals with his opponents. He has the knack of turning questions round and giving them another meaning to confuse people. He also misuses quotations by leaving out words or taking them out of context to suit himself. This was proved during the trial by researchers who went through his work with a toothcomb. Luckily, there is so much documentary evidence to prove the opposite of what he maintains that he cannot, must not, get away with it. The work of excellent historians like Deborah Lipstadt has helped to counter such denial.

I was pleased that the media gave very little publicity to the trial. Mr Irving wanted publicity and luckily did not get it. During the trial, he was scarcely mentioned on television or radio. Only the broadsheet newspapers covered the proceedings, and they were usually very critical of Mr Irving. The popular press ignored him completely. This was very impor-

---

2. Deborah Lipstadt, *Denying the Holocaust* (London: Penguin Books Ltd, 1994), p. 103.

tant because certainly one of the main reasons he brought the trial was to publicise his case.

I knew David Irving many years ago when I worked in the Wiener Library in London, then the most important Holocaust library in the world. He came to the library to carry out research for his first book. He was very polite, well spoken, good-looking, and always gave donations to the library – but for some reason neither I nor anyone else on the library staff felt comfortable with him. Only when his first book was published did we realise where he stood.

He was completely discredited as a historian following the trial. He has been banned from Germany, Canada and several other countries. Sadly, he is still allowed to preach his beliefs in America where many people support him and give him money.

## Why do you think that far-right political parties have been so successful in former East Germany? (16-year-old, Germany)

The popularity of far-right parties in former East Germany is most probably due to disillusionment, and has economic roots.

When the unification of East and West Germany took place in 1990, people in East Germany thought they would soon have the same standard of living as the West Germans. But such changes do not happen quickly, so people felt that nothing was changing and were frustrated. The machines in East German factories were obsolete, and there was not enough money to replace everything and bring it all up to modern standards. Factories were closed down and people became unemployed.

Let me give you an example. Jena, a beautiful East German city, specialised for many years in optical glass production. The town's factory employed 70,000 people and many other industries were dependent on it. All the products were supplied to the states behind the Iron Curtain. After unification, the manufacturer's West German branch closed down the Jena factory. Very soon only 3,000 inhabitants of Jena were still employed in the industry. The situation was desperate. Luckily, Jena has recovered extremely well over the past ten years.

In addition, until the unification of Germany, the East German Communist state system had taken care of everything. People had forgotten how to think, how to take the initiative. After unification, the only people who could take the opportunities that were available were those with sufficient initiative to break free from their education in how not to think independently.

As a result of economic frustration and lack of self-confidence, young people try to prove they are brave and powerful by taking the opportunities offered by far-right groups to attack the weakest members of society. Youth centres do offer an alternative, but I was told on a recent trip to Germany that the State has cut funding for such schemes. It is a very sad situation. Of course, this is just my subjective view.

## What do you think about the renaissance of the extreme right across Europe? (18-year-old, Germany)

It makes me both sad and angry. Sadly, many countries have failed to face up to their past. I am always pleased when I see that at least former West Germany has tried to do so. Austria was always one of the most anti-Semitic states, and it is only now trying to come to terms with what happened there during the Nazi period. The younger generation has many questions about the past, while many people from my generation (not all of them – I do not want to make sweeping generalisations) find it very difficult to talk about what happened.

Many older people find it difficult to admit that they were wrong, and to justify what they did, they look for younger people to follow them in their far-right views. They look for the young who are out of work or unsettled, and challenge them to prove their courage by desecrating cemeteries by night, or committing violent acts such as arson against foreigners' homes. Then the young people feel accepted by such groups and are given some kind of self-confidence. Mostly these people are very frightened inside and will run away from anyone who is stronger than them. Luckily, today, many people demonstrate against them, and I hope that now the anti-racist movement is in the majority.

It is closely connected with economic depression. Whenever there is a recession – and there was a very bad one when the Nazis started their campaign – people look for scapegoats: the Jews, the Armenians, the Turks, the foreigners, and so on. They say that these foreigners steal their jobs, but this is completely untrue. Countries which accept immigrants from other countries always profit by them in the end; historical studies and statistics prove it. Immigrants bring in new ideas, they work hard to establish themselves, they buy goods and this creates new jobs for others; they pay taxes, and so on.

Germany suffered a great loss by killing or exiling its Jews. Their scientists fled to other countries and helped them instead of helping Germany. Many intelligent Germans maintain that their country's culture never recovered from the loss of all the Jewish thinkers, writers, musicians, painters and so on – not just the Jews in fact, but inventive and avant-garde non-Jewish Germans as well.

I believe that the only way to counteract the far-right is to create youth organisations offering an alternative outlet to the young, occupying them with sport, art or whatever it takes to give them self-confidence.

## *I was wondering if neo-Nazis were trying to track you down? Are you safe from them? (14-year-old, England)*

A very interesting question. I do not think that I am a target for neo-Nazi groups, but of course one never knows. They have not harmed me yet and I very much hope they will not do so in the future. However, I do know one survivor whose windows were smashed and who received letters containing death-threats. It could happen to me as well, but I hope it will not.

## *What was it about the Jews that made the Germans dislike them? (13-year-old, England)*

Sadly, this was not the first time that people – not only Germans – turned against the Jews and I will try to give you a few reasons why. It was not the fault of the Jews.

One reason is religion. Jesus was a Jew, a wonderful man, who tried to help other unfortunate Jews, and thus had a large following. The ordinary people liked him too much because he gave aid to the poor and the sick. He was so popular that people in high places were afraid of him. The Christian religion has taught for centuries that the Jews killed Jesus, but in fact it was the Roman authorities because they were afraid he might incite rebellion. Crucifixion was the Roman way of killing, while the Jewish way was stoning to death.

Now if you love and respect someone like Jesus as a child, and you are told that the Jews killed him, you will think the Jews are bad people and feel prejudiced against them all your life. This is one reason why the Jews had to suffer for so many centuries.

Some other reasons: for a very long time Jews were not permitted to own land and therefore had to look for other ways of earning their living. They could not work in trades because tradesmen had to be members of the guilds and Jews were not allowed to join them. One way Jews could earn their living was by selling things, but even there they were restricted.

They became pedlars, carrying their wares from one place to the other and having to pay heavy taxes wherever they went. Jews could deal in cattle and horses, but again they were extremely heavily taxed and usually had to pay someone official to accompany them, especially in the towns.

Christians were not allowed to be moneylenders because the Bible forbade usury. But moneylenders were necessary, in the same way that banks are necessary moneylenders today. There were no such restrictions on Jews, so often they became moneylenders. However, people who owe money resent the people to whom they are in debt. The Jews were disliked and often chased out of places because the people who had borrowed money from them did not want to repay it; it was easier to force the Jews to leave than it was to pay the money back.

Later Jews became respectable bankers because they had learned how to deal with money. Many rulers in various parts of the world came to them when they needed money to run their wars. But when they did not need them any more, they often threw them out.

In schools and universities, only a small number of Jews were admitted, as there were usually quotas. Hence only the very best got in, and as a result they were often better students than the majority of the other pupils who could get in with fewer qualifications. But if you are better, then others become jealous and start to hate you. This was another reason.

Added to this was Hitler's personal hatred of Jews – we still do not know why, or how he persuaded so many people to help him in his hatred. But you can have anti-Semitism without Jews. As people generally did not meet Jews, all sorts of untrue stories could be told about them which were accepted as gospel truth. Sadly, this could happen anywhere because people are often too lazy to think and believe what they are told without questioning it.

I hope this will help you understand why Jews had to suffer so much prejudice over the years, and in many places still do.


### *What I cannot understand is why no one did anything about it. (14-year-old, England)*

In Germany at the time there were relatively few Jews – less than one per cent of the total population. The Jewish population lived mainly in the towns, and most Germans in the villages and smaller towns had never met a Jewish person in their lives. So if they were told that the Jews were devils, subhuman, vermin, many believed it because they did not know any better. If they were also told that the Jews were responsible for the famine, or the fact that there was no work, many believed it. Though some knew it was not true, they did not care what happened to the Jews, or the other people who were persecuted – Jehovah's Witnesses, homosexuals, Roma, Hitler's opponents and many others.

The other reason why people went along with Hitler's ideas was that Hitler had an army of thugs and spies, and turned children to spy on their parents and families. People were afraid of being denounced and murdered.

Yet there were instances which proved that when people joined together in opposition – even silently – they could achieve something. Let me give you an example. By 1941 there were many mixed marriages between Christian women and Jewish men. These Jewish men were made to work in factories. One morning, the Gestapo (the Nazi secret police) went to the factories after the night shift and collected them all. They imprisoned them in a hall at the Gestapo headquarters and 25 men were sent to Auschwitz. When their wives heard of these events, they took their children and stood silently in Rose Street in Berlin, in front of the building where the men were imprisoned. No one said a word. They just stood there for days and nights on end, and more and more people joined their protest. The Gestapo called out the army and lined them up opposite the women, but the soldiers refused to shoot. On the fifth day, the Gestapo let the men go and even brought back the 25 men who had been sent to Auschwitz.

As you see, when people showed a bit of civil courage and took a united stand, they did, and still do, have the power to change the course of events.


### Do you think that the British did enough to try to stop the Holocaust? (15-year-old, England)

All the free countries could have done more, if they had really wanted to. Unfortunately there was anti-Semitism in England, as in many other countries, and many people did not care what happened to the Jews. The government of the day knew that extermination camps existed, but did not permit the media to tell people about them.

They could have tried to bomb the railway lines leading to the camps, which would at least have slowed down the extermination process. They could have bombed the munitions factories, which would have brought the war to an end sooner, and fewer people would have been killed; but there were political reasons why they did not do this. One reason was that after the war with Hitler the factories would be useful in a fight against the Communists.

If Britain and other countries had allowed more refugees in, many people would have been saved. England did admit a number of immigrants, especially children in the *Kindertransports*. However, relatively few adults were allowed in, and mostly only if there were people in England willing to employ them, mainly as domestic servants or in hospitals. Many were very badly treated and used as cheap labour. Even the children often had to do very heavy work, were treated harshly and were sometimes abused. But many were treated well and it certainly saved the lives of all.

Then at the start of the war, most of the refugees were interned. No distinction was made between German Nazis living in this country and German Jewish refugees who had already been ill-treated by the Nazis. They were all put in camps together on the Isle of Man. Some were even sent to Australia and Canada, and many perished when their boats were torpedoed. On the boats they were treated much worse than the other internees. As no one in these countries was told that they were refugees from the Nazi regime, only that they were of German origin, they often suffered much persecution.

## Why didn't you emigrate into a liberal country like the US at the first sign of persecution? (17-year-old, Germany)

Firstly, the Jews had been persecuted so often and for so long that people accepted it as part of life. The first restrictions did not ring any warning bells because we had learned to live with anti-Semitism.

Secondly, other countries were not so keen to take us in. Some admitted a few refugees at the beginning of the persecution, but they stopped or made it so difficult that it was effectively impossible. To give you an example of the prejudice we faced, at the Evian Conference on refugees in 1938, the Australians said they had no anti-Semitism in their country; they would not take Jews so as not to create any.

My mother was born in Austria and would have been eligible to join the Austrian quota of refugees to the US, and I could have gone with her as I was a minor. Sadly, our quota number did not become valid until 1942, by which time Hungary had declared war against the US and we could no longer leave. I myself also tried to go to Palestine with a group of Zionist friends, but did not manage it, even when I later tried to get out illegally. As you see, it was not that simple.

Some people did not even try to leave because they didn't believe things would really deteriorate so much; they still had faith in humanity. Others hoped they would be lucky and weather it out. Emigration is a big step. If you have worked hard all your life to create a home and own a house or business, it is not easy to give everything up – especially if you cannot even take with you the money from the sale of your property (which could only have been sold at a great loss anyway). By the time people understood that it was a matter of life and death, it was too late. There was nowhere to go.

### What do you think was so intimidating about the Nazis which held the Jewish people back from violent resistance? (14-year-old, England)

Simple: machine-guns! The Jews were basically not a violent people. In Hungary all the Jewish men between the ages of 18 and 50 had to join the army. Hence, the only Jews left were women, children and old men. (When I was young, anyone over 50 was considered old!) We certainly had no access to arms, nor were we trained to use them. We had strength in numbers, but what can people do when they are faced with even just a few men armed with machine-guns? At any sign of opposition they would have mowed us down. We were also faced with the Hungarian police who were armed and quite willing to co-operate with the Nazis. We were in a state of shock. What could we have done?

The other reason we did not resist was that the Nazis used the 'salami-technique' of introducing restrictions one small step at a time. We always hoped that the latest measure would be the last. Each time things got a little bit worse, we said, 'This is still bearable,' and by the time it became quite unbearable, we had been stripped of everything. When we were deported, the rumours we heard reassured us that the old people would look after the children and sick, and do the cooking, and the younger ones would have to do hard labour, but if they worked hard there would be no danger. We believed it because we wanted to believe it. It is very difficult to credit how inhumane man can be towards his fellow human beings. Also because we had no television, we didn't see emaciated people or starving children, and could not imagine man's inhumanity towards his fellow human beings.

By the time we really understood what was happening, it was too late. We were surrounded. We had no way out. As Pastor Niemoeller said, 'There was no one left to speak out for me.'

Do I think the Jewish people did all they could to resist? My answer to your question would be 'No'. People could have emigrated earlier, though they had to find a country to let them in, and this was difficult. We could have fought back, but it would have meant certain death. The resistance fighters in the Warsaw ghetto gave up life once they started to resist. It was an honourable death, but death it was. And I believed in life and survival, though not at any price, only as long as I could keep my integrity.

## What led you to do sabotage work? (16-year-old, Germany)

One of the reasons was that if we prevented the bombs from working, we might be able to shorten the war, which would give us a better chance of surviving. There were many other such sabotage groups. Not much research has been done on the subject; and I am hoping that one day someone will write a detailed study of all the different types of sabotage that went on.

## What do you think the German soldiers would have thought of it? Don't you think it was unfair to the German soldiers when you did sabotage work as a way of resisting? (16-year-old, Germany)

I am sorry, but we were not at all interested in what the German soldiers would have thought. We were just trying to end the war more quickly. After all, the war was started by Germany. We had to help those who were fighting to help us, or at least were on our side. Sabotage was our way of resisting: we could not fight empty-handed against machine-guns.

Yes, it was unfair on those who only fought to defend their country. But there were many soldiers who attacked unarmed people – who shot children, women and old people into mass graves. Later in the camps, we were guarded by soldiers who made our lives as miserable as they could. It was not unfair to sabotage weapons used by such people.

## Why have the Jews received compensation, but no Black people, Indians or Chinese have had any? (18-year-old, Germany)

Before the Holocaust, no one had ever tried systematically to eliminate an entire race. Even those victims who were not exterminated on arrival at the camps were intended to be exploited for their strength and then destroyed. The Nazis called it 'extermination through work' – and this took place in the most civilised country in the world.

Afterwards, Germany realised it had done something inhuman and for its own sake felt it should compensate those who had suffered. West Germany was the first country to face up to its past, even if it took a very long time to happen. Gradually, other countries started compensation schemes, but Hungarian compensation is more of an insult than anything else.

No one attempted to exterminate Indian, Chinese or black people. However, they were exploited, used as slave-workers and many were killed by their colonisers, and they should be compensated. Only the people concerned can fight for compensation.

World War II ended in 1945. It is now the twenty-first century and we are only just starting to see the fruits of our struggle for compensation. Even then, how can one possibly compensate properly for people's lives being ruined? How does one calculate what a life is worth? The most important thing is the recognition of guilt.

Many injustices have been done in the world, but mostly these were and are internal or tribal affairs, where one tribe wants to rule over the other. The Holocaust was different. This is how I see it, though my knowledge of other countries' internal affairs is limited.

## What other kinds of resistance were there? (18-year-old, England)

I am not able to tell you much about resistance in Auschwitz-Birkenau, where I was taken first. I did not know personally about the crematorium oven being blown up, but it is a well-documented event.

I was not religious myself, but some people tried to resist by carrying out some sort of religious service and keeping the festivals, even fasting at Yom Kippur. I suppose this could be considered a form of resistance because people tried to assert their Jewishness in the face of the enemy.

Some of us denied that we understood or spoke German. In fact it was my mother tongue; my mother spoke only rather bad Hungarian, so I always spoke German with her. In camp I denied any knowledge of German and nearly paid with my life for doing so. Can this be considered passive resistance? I suppose it could be taken as such.

I remember another small incident which could be called resistance. While working on the conveyor belt, along with some German women, we were often told to sing. As I had a pleasant voice, I sometimes started the singing. On one occasion I began with quite a popular German song, the *Lorelei*, which I knew had been banned in Germany because its composer, Mendelssohn, was Jewish. All the German women were thrilled and we sang away. One woman even remarked how long it was since she had heard this song and was really pleased; she wanted us to sing it again, and so we started. Suddenly a foreman came and shouted furiously at us to stop. I had my moment of triumph – I was pleased. Could this be considered resistance because I knew the song was banned?

There was of course our sabotage group in Hessisch-Lichtenau, and in fact there was another group in the camp at the same time, although we were not aware of its existence then.

### Have you read Anne Frank's diaries? What do you think of them? (14-year-old, Germany)

Yes, I have read Anne Frank's diaries and found them very moving. In her diaries Anne still believes in the goodness of humanity. This was before she was deported to Auschwitz, and then to Belsen where she subsequently died.

And Anne's is not the only diary of a young person in the Holocaust. There is a book called *Children's Wartime Diaries*, edited by Laurel Holliday, which is a collection of writings by young people who were affected by the Holocaust.

### Do you think that books sometimes cannot put across how horrific it must have been? (14-year-old, England)

I have been telling my story to students for the past 14 years and most, if not all, say that they understand what happened much better through hearing the story than by reading about it in books. I must accept that it is true. Books talk about events in general terms, about numbers like six million, which are sometimes just too large and abstract to comprehend fully. A personal account brings home the truth much better. There are numerous, moving personal accounts available nowadays.

Nevertheless it is also important to read books. The historian's task is to compare many facts and decide which are valid and which are important, so it is necessary to read as widely and critically as possible.

### Have you seen Schindler's List, and if so what did you think of it? (14-year-old, England)

I saw the film and was extremely moved by it. Some people say it was too 'Hollywoodised', meaning that it did not really show the true horrors and was somehow sweetened. I do not agree. I found that most of the time it was as true to events as a non-documentary film could possibly be. After all, the director Steven Spielberg could not have made actors as emaciated as people were under those circumstances. I believe it was a very valuable film; it caught the public imagination. Since then, people are willing to listen to what really happened and invite survivors to speak out. Earlier, most people did not want to know.

To me, the film basically shows how the character of Oskar Schindler changed. At the beginning, he is a selfish, nasty businessman, with an eye for the main chance, trying to make money out of slave-labour. But when he has contact with his slave-labourers, he realises that they are human beings and does all he can to save their lives. It is the opposite of the film *Mephisto*, which shows how a decent human being can be manipulated through fear, ambition and propaganda into a vicious collaborator.

I don't think that anyone who saw *Schindler's List* really considered it as entertainment. When people went to see it, they were so moved that at the end they sat through the credits in perfect silence; and they were still silent when they walked out of the cinema. I never saw this happen with any other film.

***What other good films are there on the Holocaust? Have any of them tried to pretend it was better than what really happened? (14-year-old, England)***

There are many Holocaust films and documentaries. Claude Lanzmann's *Shoah* is certainly the most true and powerful of them all; it is mainly documentary footage and interviews with victims, perpetrators and bystanders. But it is nine hours long and most people do not have the patience, or find it too much, too honest, to bear.

Some documentaries, like the TV series called *Holocaust*, have been rather 'Hollywoodised'. But *Holocaust* still had its uses. In Germany, it was the first film on the Holocaust to make a big impact and people started to ask questions and wanted to know more. Until then, there was silence.

I am sure there have also been films made to minimise what happened, but I don't think I have seen any. There are some things which have always been omitted. I have never seen a film (as opposed to a documentary) which portrayed the death-marches, the killing of children or medical experiments on human beings. But most people cannot take these things and would refuse to watch.

If the reality of the Holocaust is only brought home to people in documentaries, it will only register with an elite; others will switch off. But people are willing to watch films with a story-line and will remember them, so in my opinion, it is better to have such films than not, even if sometimes it devalues the reality.

There are also some wonderful films like *The Music Box, The Shop on the Corner, The Escape from Sobibor, Night and Fog,* and others. One can learn from these. *Life is Beautiful* was not a Holocaust film: it was a love story where the ultimate, namely the Holocaust, has been brought in to prove the love.

### *Is the representation – documentary or artistic – of extreme suffering ethically justified? (University student, England)*

This is a very complicated question and I think that one has to judge every case individually.

In my opinion, documentary representation is certainly warranted if it is done for educational reasons, rather than for cheap sensationalism. If, for instance, it can help to prevent future suffering, then it is most necessary. But it must be done extremely sensitively so as not to cause even more distress.

One case in which it is certainly ethical is if seeing, reading or talking about such things can help to release tension for those who have suffered. Being able to discuss painful things openly has a healing capacity, and this is certainly very valid.

I think that the same criteria apply to artistic representation. Of course, in addition, the more sensitively the facts are represented, the more successful the finished work of art will be.

### *Is it true that there is a play based on your life? (University student, England)*

Some years ago, I read a book by Victoria Ancona Vincent, who was deported to Auschwitz from Milan. She lived in Nottingham, was in a wheelchair and never spoke about her experiences, or even about being Jewish. She married an English Christian. When Beth Shalom Holocaust Centre opened in Laxton, Nottinghamshire, she read about it and decided that she wanted to go there. From then on, she started to speak and Beth Shalom's director, Dr Stephen Smith, arranged for her to visit schools and speak to students at the Holocaust Centre. He also persuaded her to write down her story and published it under the title *Beyond Imagination*. As I also spoke regularly at Beth Shalom, I often heard of her and she heard of me, but we never met.

When I read her book, I realised that although we had never met, we were on the same death-march. I sent Victoria a message through Beth Shalom. She became very excited and wanted very much to meet me. We met twice at Beth Shalom and then sadly she died. The story of our meeting is the basis of a play called *Across the Bridge*. This was performed first at Beth Shalom in September 1997, then in Jerusalem at the Yad Vashem Holocaust Memorial Centre, and finally for two weeks in London, at the New End Theatre in Hampstead. It was a great success, and there are many plans for its future.

## Why is your autobiography called A Cat Called Adolf? (14-year-old, Germany)

I returned to Germany for the first time in 1984. My husband and I were on holiday in Scandinavia, and we decided to travel back through Germany in order to stay with a South African friend of mine, who had been inviting us for many years to stay at her weekend home in the Lüneburger Heide.

I asked my friend to make sure that I would not have to meet people my age or older. I didn't want to run the risk of shaking hands with the people who murdered my family or friends, or anyone else. Nonetheless we did meet two people from that generation.

The first was a man who had been a prisoner-of-war in Russia throughout the period, and only heard about the Holocaust when he returned to Germany in 1948. The second was a delightful old lady who ran a grocery store. When we went to the store for provisions, she could not have been more pleasant and helpful. One day, my husband felt he wanted to buy some green beans; she had none in the shop, but gave us some of her own as a gift since she was a friend of our hosts. She also took us into her garden to give us lettuce and herbs.

It was a very hot day, and there were many cats in her house. Suddenly she said, 'Look at that cat; we call him Adolf because he always lifts his paw up as if he's making the '*Heil-Hitler*' salute!'

That was the first time I had agreed to stay in Germany for more than one day, and I had constantly been expecting something unpleasant to happen. But the people had been charming, friendly and helpful, so I could not be angry with them. Now it had happened. It felt like I had been hit on the head with a sledgehammer. I looked at my watch and made an excuse to leave.

When my husband and I were outside, I told him that I wanted to leave Germany straight away; I didn't wish to stay in a country where a cat that raised its paw was nicknamed Adolf. And that is the reason for the title of my book. My husband told me later that while we were going through the house, he saw a photograph of two men in SS uniforms very prominently displayed.

**What do you think about Holocaust museums? I recently spoke to a lady whose father was a survivor of the Holocaust. While wholeheartedly supporting Holocaust museums, she also explained that the museums exposed feelings which she had ignored, and also feelings she wasn't even aware she had. (University student, England)**

I have not seen many Holocaust museums, but the ones I have seen are impressive. For me, the main purpose of such museums is to educate people. They are also memorials to those who perished and to the communities that disappeared or nearly disappeared. I suppose that Holocaust museums are also memorials to those who lived through the Holocaust and survived. Museums have a most important role because people still persist in trying to deny that the Holocaust happened. Their exhibitions and archives provide incontrovertible proof against Holocaust denial.

Beth Shalom Holocaust Centre in Nottinghamshire is really quite exceptional, not least because it was founded by a non-Jewish family. It certainly fulfils all the criteria for success. The exhibition is excellent and very moving; it gives a good background to Jewish history and then carries on through to today. Groups of students, from age 13 upwards, go to visit every day. They see the exhibition, with a small historical introduction, and hear a survivor speaking. They can browse in the library and visit the memorial gardens. Beth Shalom also organises conferences, seminars for teachers and artistic events; it publishes individual memoirs, encourages young theatre groups with relevant productions and sponsors productions at the Centre. It also supports artists producing work relating to the Holocaust.

Two other museums I have seen, Yad Vashem in Jerusalem and the United States Holocaust Memorial Museum in Washington, are both much larger. The Washington Holocaust Museum has a purpose-built building and has been packed and sold out every day since it opened. Approximately 2.5 million people visit it every year, which must have some influence. The exhibition is in chronological sequence, as in Beth Shalom, but extends over three floors with much more space. There is an impressive number of photographs and artefacts, and even an entire cattle-truck. It also has a large education department, guided tours, archive, library and research department - all excellent.

But what my husband and I found most impressive was a continuously running film of survivors describing their experiences. It contains a massive amount of material, and though we spent three days there, we did not have enough time to see it from beginning to end. There were many groups from schools all over the United States, and the pupils were very much taken aback by what they saw. And this is the main value of all these places, even though they are valuable already in themselves.

My husband left Berlin when he was 16 with a group of youngsters, and was taken to a children's village in Palestine. He never saw his parents again. On our first day at the Washington museum, he recognised one of his childhood friends on a photograph of a train leaving Berlin, bound for Palestine. It was at approximately the same date as my husband left Berlin and he was extremely moved. In the archive we found where the picture came from, and we wrote to see if they had any idea what had happened to this youngster - now an old man - but we never received an answer. However, it meant a lot to my husband to see a picture of his childhood friend.

Yad Vashem in Jerusalem was the first Holocaust museum to be founded and is quite different. The archive and library are less satisfactory, but the exhibits are really imaginative. Much of the museum is outdoors. There are memorials to communities and an extremely impressive hall as a memorial to children: visitors are led through passages in the dark and can only see stars, while there is a continuous roll-call of the names of children who perished in the Holocaust.

There is also an extremely moving memorial hall with an everlasting light for the millions of people murdered in camps. Yad Vashem is visited by groups of youngsters from the Israeli Army, schools and universities, and after their visit you see them sitting outside with their group leader, discussing what they saw, and you can see what an enormous impact it has made on them.

What is most important in all these museums is that school children and youngsters are brought from great distances to see them, and they have guided tours and questionnaires to encourage them to consider what the visit has meant to them.

Sometimes, when I speak about my experiences, I feel that I am a bit of a museum exhibit myself – even if I'm not in a museum at the time! But I also feel that what I say touches people. I get letters and even poems written to me, with or without additional questions. I promise the young people I speak to that if they write with questions they will receive a full individual reply, a promise which I always keep.

The Imperial War Museum in London opened a Holocaust Museum in 2000. For me, any Holocaust Museum is only as valuable as its Education Department, so I am very pleased that theirs is excellent. It has outstanding exhibits and the videos relating survivors' experiences are extremely moving. The history of the Nazi era is told in good chronological order, with ample textual explanation, many good posters and many artefacts. There is much more material than can be absorbed in an hour and a half, which is the time usually allocated to student groups.

The Jewish Museum in London also has an Education Department and a small permanent exhibition about the experiences of an English Jew, Leon Greenman, during his deportation. In Germany I have seen a number of smaller memorials, limited in space but still with impressive exhibitions, which are all extremely active and successful in education.

### How do you think we should plan for the future of Holocaust education? (17-year-old, England)

I am very much involved in Holocaust education, not only by telling my story but also by writing articles and discussing different types of education with various bodies. We survivors watch films which will be suitable to show after we are no longer here to say what is true. We publish our memoirs. We allow ourselves to be filmed so these eye-witness accounts can be shown in schools, because we find that in Holocaust museums people find personal accounts the most moving. They bring the Holocaust down to the voices of individual people.

It is also most important that we relate our experience to what is happening today. Some people say that the Holocaust was just another genocide, even if it was the most brutal and premeditated of them all. When I tell my story, I try to demonstrate how this genocide was different by beginning with a quotation from a book by Bernice Rubens called *The Brothers*:

> But why is this holocaust more offensive, more foul, more malignant, more grievous than anything that has happened in history before?
> It is not a question of numbers.
> Millions of black people have been slaughtered in their history.

Millions of aborigines.

Who can count the Armenians?

Who dare count the American Indians?

No. Not numbers.

This genocide is different from all others. It is different because of its sublime and obscene efficiency. Mass murder when not a minute is lost. Mass burial where nothing is wasted.

Human skin for reading lamps.

Human flesh for soap.

Human hair for pillows.

Man's teeth for investment.

No waste.

It is a system meticulous in every detail, long pre-meditated, planned and co-ordinated, administered with the most sophisticated and satanic technology.

It is an artistry of murder, that achieves a certain beauty in its symmetry.

That is the core of its obscenity. That is why it is different.

In the whole history of murdering man, among all its victimised peoples, there has never been a more accomplished, a more ingenious, a more cunning or more terrible cavalcade of cruelty.

Dear God, let no one ever forget this, ever, ever, ever.[3]

And the last piece of evidence I show is a document showing the SS's calculations of the profitability of slave-labourers. Nothing was wasted, right down to their bones and ashes. I cannot prove it but I do believe that no similar document exists in connection with any other genocide.

When talking about the Holocaust, we must remember the other victims – the Gypsies, Jehovah's Witnesses, homosexuals, the Poles and Russians, and Hitler's political opponents – who also suffered. Then we have to talk about other genocides as well. There is no hierarchy of suffering; dead is dead is dead. And there is also the problem of asylum-seekers. After my liberation, I did not return to Hungary because they had behaved so abominably, and so I became stateless from 1945 to 1957, that is, for 12 years. A stateless person has no papers, is an outcast. I had no work permit, but still had to eat and have a roof over my head, so I worked illegally.

The British Government instituted an annual Holocaust Memorial Day on 27 January 2001. An excellent teaching-pack was prepared and

---

3. Bernice Rubens, *The Brothers* (Edinburgh: Hamish Hamilton, 1983), pp. 360–1.

---

### SS Profitability Calculations
### on the Exploitation of Concentration Camp Inmates

| | | |
|---|---|---|
| Daily average leasing wages | RM | 6.-- |
| less food | RM | -.60 |

average life expectancy 9 months:

| | | |
|---|---|---|
| 9 months = 270 x RM 5.30 = | RM | 1,431.-- |
| less clothing   write-off | RM | -.10 |

Proceeds from efficient utilisation of the corpse :

| | |
|---|---|
| 1. Gold  teeth | 3. Valuables |
| 2. Clothing | 4. Money |

| | | |
|---|---|---|
| less cost of cremation | RM | 2.-- |
| average net profit | RM | 200.-- |
| Total profit after 9 months | RM | 1,631,-- |

plus proceeds from utilisation of bones and ash

---

FGURE 7: SS Profitability Calculations on the Exploitation of Concentration Camp Inmates. From Berndt Klemitz, Die Arbeitssklaven der Dynamit-Nobel [The Slave-Labourers of Dynamit-Nobel] (Engelbrecht, 1980, p. 191).

launched, because it only makes sense to have this day if it is really used to educate people. There are a number of teaching manuals in existence: the most extensive is the one produced by the Spiro Institute (now London Jewish Cultural Centre) and the Holocaust Educational Trust.

When people ask me what lessons should be learnt from the Holocaust, I always advise them: firstly, try not to generalise, because people are all individuals. Secondly, try to understand and respect other religions and cultures, and try not to think that only your own is valid.

## What would you do to prevent something like the Holocaust happening again? (14-year-old, England)

First of all, what I am already doing: relating my story to as many people, young and old, as are willing to listen.

Then, to remind people of the saying of the Jewish sage Hillel: 'What is hateful unto you, do not do unto your neighbour.' If people remember this, they cannot hurt others. You would not like to be hit or have injustice inflicted upon you, so you should not attack other people or treat them unjustly.

We need to teach people to evaluate what they hear, and not take things at face value. And it is important to be tolerant, to accept that other people may have different ideas. As long as they do not harm anyone, they have the right to think differently.

## I would like to ask you why you think in this day and age some people aren't treated equally among others? (15-year-old, England)

This is a very good question and certainly not easy to answer in a few words. However, I shall try to write down some thoughts about it.

People are not all the same; some are small, some are big; some are white, some are yellow or black; some are brainy, while others are less clever. Some grow up in a house full of books, others in homes where the parents are illiterate. Some are born with every advantage, while others have to struggle for everything they wish to attain and may not have the physical or moral strength to get there.

Then there is the fact that different people with different backgrounds are often brought up with different values. Some cultures accept acts which others strictly forbid, and this goes for religions as well. If we try to acquaint ourselves with other people's cultures, we will understand each other much better.

There are people who have been hurt in some way at some time, or are envious of others and become aggressive. They may feel inferior, and as a way of hiding it, may bully and oppress less fortunate people, to show how much stronger they are. It is really very cowardly to oppress people who are in the minority and therefore weaker, but some people feel they have to do it to prove how strong and powerful they are. I suppose we must listen to such people and try to understand why they need to show off, so that we can try to help them, though sometimes this is very difficult.

107

There is one thing we all have, and that is free will to decide how we think and behave towards others. It is also a matter of self-respect. Sometimes it takes courage to think differently from others, but if you believe that it is right, then you should try to stick to your beliefs, principles and ideals – not just follow unthinkingly because it is sometimes difficult to be different. I try to respect everyone, just as I expect others to respect me. But respect has to be earned and proven by actions.

## Do you yourself have prejudices against minorities? (14-year-old, Germany)

I try not to have any prejudices against anyone. It is important not to make generalisations about groups as a whole, but to judge the individual case. Sometimes I do catch myself making generalisations without thinking, and then I am very angry with myself and make myself stop.

## How do you feel when you see people still being murdered for what they believe in? (14-year-old, England)

We Jews were not murdered for what we believed in, but because we were born Jewish. My family were not religious, but believed in being decent human beings, tolerating and helping others. We were not deported for our beliefs; even people who grew up as Christians but had two Jewish grandparents were considered Jewish and taken to the concentration camps.

One and a half million children were murdered during the Holocaust and many of them were far too young to have any belief in anything. They were murdered solely for being the children of Jews or any other of Hitler's targets. The persecution had nothing to do with belief.

Hitler's political opponents, partisans and Jehovah's Witnesses, however, *were* all murdered for their beliefs during the Nazi era. Terrorists or freedom fighters (depending on how you regard them) scare me just as much as fundamentalists of any creed. Sometimes I also feel sorry for them because they are often used as pawns in other people's power games.

I feel very upset and angry when people are indiscriminately murdered for any reason, and certainly when whole groups are killed just because they were born into a particular nationality, religion or colour.

*Do you feel that since the war people have learnt to treat other people as equals? (14-year-old, England)*

No, they have not. But then people are not all the same. People do have different values, cultures and religions. As long as they do not harm anyone, there is nothing wrong with people being different. On the contrary, we can learn from each other.

It makes me very sad that people still despise others because they are in some way different, instead of learning about their differences and trying to respect them. We need to learn to evaluate everything we hear, not accept unthinkingly what others say. We need to learn to weigh the consequences of our words and deeds.

Often this takes some courage, but the more people who understand this and are prepared to take action, the easier it becomes to create a society with decent values.

*Do you think that giving your talks has helped you to come to terms with your experiences? (University student, England)*

I do not really know. After the war I immediately wrote down some of my experiences and also spoke straight away if there was someone who wanted to listen. Later, from 1959 to 1964, I worked in the Wiener Library in London, which was the only Holocaust library in the world at that time. I was constantly confronted with material dealing with the Holocaust and I started speaking quite early, long before it became a definite part of the curriculum in schools. I was asked to speak to teachers who took part in yearly conferences on race-relations. I was asked to speak to university students who took a course at Southampton University on the Holocaust – this was also an annual event. It was only after *Schindler's List* came out in 1994 that schools invited us or allowed us to speak to students. By that time I had come to terms with what had happened to me. Also, because in my case many things went terribly wrong after the war, the main reason I wrote my book was to show that if you survived, it was not the end. The physical and psychological consequences continued, and still continue. Hence I am not sure how much it has helped me.

*What gives you the strength to go on? (18-year-old, Germany)*

I'm not quite sure. I grew up in a family with lots of ideals and principles. They are extremely important to me as well. I have also managed nearly all my life to keep my integrity and my self-respect even when it endangered my life. Except for one occasion when I failed, my entire life I have tried to remain a decent human being. This was the most important thing for me. To respect my fellow human beings – as long as they deserved respect – whether they were Christians, Moslems, Buddhists, yellow, black, English, Irish, Polish, Germans or Jews. Having a sense of humour has helped, and also friendships.

### Did you have any personal role models and ideals? (18-year-old, Germany)

Yes, my parents, who were always extremely decent human beings. And also people like Pablo Casals, the world-renowned cellist, who refused to return to Spain because of Franco's repressive regime; Picasso, the well-known painter and sculptor; Bela Bartok, the Hungarian pianist and composer, who left Hungary because he did not want to live in a fascist dictatorship; Marlene Dietrich, who took a stand against Hitler's regime; Thomas Mann, the most important German writer of that period. All these people were Christians and did not need to flee; they showed the world that they had a conscience and a strong character, and did not allow themselves to be sucked in with the mob or be influenced by ambition or fear. These are only a few. I could mention many others who were not famous. They all had civil courage.

### What has stayed with you most about the experience (in any respect – memory, knowledge, feelings towards people/situations etc.)? (University student, England)

This is a difficult one; the word 'most' makes it so. The dehumanisation. The realisation that I was very much an individualist.

Before the war I wanted to emigrate to Palestine. I tried legally and I tried illegally, but I did not succeed. I wanted to go into a kibbutz, become a pioneer. After the war I knew that I would not fit into that kind of life; I was too much of an individualist. Hence I did not aim for Palestine because I did not realise I could have gone and worked in a town. I did this later when I lived there – by then it was Israel – from 1949 to 1951, nearly two years. In spite of having a terribly difficult time there, I loved it and left only for a visit to South Africa for family reasons, but was then unable to return because of practical reasons. I was very homesick for

Israel, which I never was for Hungary where they treated us abominably.

There were many things that remained, like trusting people, which I still occasionally find difficult; physical things like sitting on a sandy beach which I am unable to do as it always reminds me of the porous soil we sat on in the camp, which stuck to us; going to a public swimming place where sometimes many women shower naked, not because I am a prude but because it reminds me of when we had to stand naked. I feel sick if anyone stands next to me with body odour.

## Could you say that you are happy now? (University student, England)

Yes, reasonably happy. But I am lucky to have a nature where I mostly see the good side and not the bad. My cup is half full not half empty.

## What do you think of the whole past and how did you feel telling us about your past? (15-year-old, England)

It makes me feel frustrated, angry and sad that these things could happen; that civilised people could behave thus to their fellow human beings. It makes me feel even angrier, sadder and more helpless that somewhat similar deeds are happening all the time and we still take action much too late. Since today news arrives faster, and television, which we did not have at the time of the Holocaust, allows us to see injustices as they happen, in an ideal or 'civilised' world things should have changed.

People need to learn to tolerate others; maybe then they would not kill each other. I recently met a young Serbian and also a young Albanian from Kosovo, who had both left their countries and become asylum-seekers. They were forced to join their country's armies, but neither of them was willing to do so. They had friends of other nationalities and other religions and might have been obliged to kill them. They refused and therefore had to flee. I am very happy that Britain gave them refuge.

I feel that I have to relate what happened to us in the Holocaust in the hope it will make you think about why such things happen, and how they can be prevented from happening again. I hope it will help you think about how you would feel if it happened to you.

Evaluate whether charismatic people – people who look good and speak fluently – are really saying something valuable, meaningful and unambiguous, or just seeking power. Learn not to generalise, not to talk about the Jews, the Gypsies, the Irish, the English or the Hottentots, because people are all individuals with individual feelings and sensibilities and moral values. If I can make this understood a little, then I have not spoken in vain.

## What do you expect of the young people of today? (21-year-old, Germany)

That they should learn to think and not be too lazy to do so: it is a gift which only mankind has and it makes us different from all other living beings. That they should evaluate carefully when listening to people like Hitler, who had charisma but expressed false and dangerous ideas, and not follow such leaders uncritically. Millions of Germans perished in World War I. In spite of this, after a short period of only 20 years' peace, Germany embarked on a new war without thought for the consequences. Not only were six million Jews and millions of others killed in this war, but thousands of German soldiers and civilians also lost their lives. If people had been thinking, all this could possibly have been avoided. I expect, or at least hope, that the young people of today will become decent, upright human beings who don't think only of themselves, but recognise that others have the same right to a decent life. I hope they will also learn that in every culture and civilisation, there are many good and valuable elements, and that one should not despise people because they are different. They must also learn not to generalise because peoples are made up of individuals and if one takes the trouble, it is very interesting to get to know other cultures.

## What wishes do you have, personally and generally, for a modern, conscious society, a society of the future? (21-year-old, Germany)

The world doesn't stand still. Since the beginning of history, there have always been migrations of nations. People change habitats; some in their own country, some just because they are looking for a different environment, many for various reasons connected with politics, wars, persecutions or poverty. Many were taken from their own countries to work and help the economic development of other countries. Some of these have eventually returned to their country of origin, but many have settled and built up families, and their children were born and grew up in the new country. Most countries have integrated these immigrants into their society after a certain period. There have also been many mixed marriages, and, sadly, raping of women over the thousands of years; there is no such thing as a pure race. Each new person brings something of his or her old culture; it makes the receiving countries more interesting, healthier and less degenerate. It is a question of give-and-take. In each group there are better and less good people because they are all individuals and not the same as each other. There are people who are shy or aggressive, caring or selfish, in all variations and in all societies. And this is why it is so important never to generalize because one cannot speak of the Jews, the Gypsies, the Germans, the English, the Blacks, the Orientals, the Christians or the Muslims, and so on, only as groups.

When I'm speaking to German groups in Germany, I am often asked what I think of the Germans. I always say that as far as I am concerned, there is no such thing. Even the Germans of my generation were not all pleased about what was happening there or with Hitler's ideas. There were also many courageous Germans who cared about the Jews and others who were persecuted, who hid them, fed them and helped them. The second generation had nothing to do with the persecutions, and the third generation even less. These younger generations should not feel guilt for what their forefathers did, but should learn about what happened, think about it and ensure that it never happens again. So, one must never generalize. Of course it is not only the Germans who should learn this, but all other nations as well. It is dangerous to generalize; we all do it, but I have tried to train myself never to do it because it leads to trouble. If someone in a group wins the Nobel prize or a gold medal for something he or she has achieved, it doesn't mean that everyone in that group is a high-achiever. And if someone in a group is a thief or a fraud, it doesn't make all the group into thieves and frauds. If we think hard about this and try to accept people as they are (except when they are crooks or murderers) and learn to respect others, the world could be a different place; only then could we live together in peace. There is so much beauty in this world, why spoil it?

*If you could put your message into a few sentences, what would it be? (21-year-old, Germany)*

I urge you to think and evaluate everything you hear and not to let yourself be influenced by people because they have a charismatic voice. Don't believe everything without looking at it critically. You are individuals and must make up your minds about your beliefs as upright, honest people, and follow your principles even if it is sometimes dangerous. If many people do this together, it has at least a chance of achieving good results.

# Bibliography

## Publications of Dr Trude Levi

### Books

*The Gaster Papers: A Biographical List*, The Library of University College London, Occasional Publications, No. 2 (London: The Library of University College, London, 1976).
*A Cat Called Adolf* [autobiography] (London: Vallentine Mitchell, 1995).
*Eine Katze Namens Adolf* [autobiography] Birgit Jessen (transl.) (Witzenhausen: Ekopan, 1997).

### Short Stories

'Kashruth in the Castle', *AJR Information* (April, 1995).
'Kashruth in the Castle,' 'The Story of a Beloved Granddaughter,' and 'The Ultimate Sunrise', *Out of the Dark: A Volume of Short Stories of Survivors*, selected by Alan Sillitoe (London: Jewish Care/Holocaust Survivors' Centre, 1997), pp. 57, 84, 123.
'Progress', 'The Vineyard', 'Return' [article], *Into the Light: More Short Stories* [and articles] *by Survivors*, Foreword by Alan Sillitoe (London: Holocaust Survivors' Centre, 2000), pp. 98–112, 119–24, 125–37.
'Nature's Theatre', *The Holocaust Survivors' Centre News* (Spring 1999), p. 23.
'A Haircut', *The Holocaust Survivors' Centre News* (2000), p. 27.

### Articles

'The Gaster Papers', *Miscellanies Part X, Sessions 1973–1975, Transactions of the Jewish Historical Society of England*, 25 (1977), p. 252.
'Selected and Classified Bibliography for 1983', in William Frankel (ed.), *Survey of Jewish Affairs* (Rutherford/Madison/Teaneck/Fairleigh Dickinson: Associated University Presses, 1985), pp. 276–308.

'Selected and Classified Bibliography for 1985', in William Frankel (ed.), *Survey of Jewish Affairs* (Rutherford/Madison/Teaneck/Fairleigh Dickinson: Associated University Presses, 1985), pp. 235–67.

'Forty Years After: A Memoir', *The Wiener Library Newsletter*, 1 (April 1985) pp.3–4.

'Forty Years After: A Memoir', *Multicultural Teaching*, 5, 2 (Spring 1987), pp. 4–5. [Illustrated and extended version of the above.]

'The Jewish Material at University College London, Libraries and archives', in Judith Joseph (ed.), *Proceedings of the Second International Genealogical Seminar on Jewish Genealogy, London, July 1987. Birmingham, UK* (International Jewish Genealogical Resources, 1988).

'Der Todesmarsch aus Leipzig nach Riesa. Aus den Aufzeichnungen von Gertrud Deak' [later Trude Levi], in Manfred Unger and Hubert Lang (eds), *Juden in Leipzig. Eine Dokumentation zur Ausstellung anlässlich des 50. Jahrestages der Faschistischen Pogromnacht ... vom 5. November bis 17. Dezember 1988* (Leipzig: Rat des Bezirkes, Abteilung Kultur, p. 202) [transl. from Hungarian].

'The Judaica Collection at University College London, 1990', Paper given at The Jewish Heritage Conference, Southampton University, July 1990. Dr Kadish Sharman (ed.), To be published.

'The Ultimate Sunrise', *Ruach* (May 1997), p. 25.

'The Cattle Truck', *Ruach* (June 1997), p. 21.

'On Talking about the Holocaust', *Ruach* (September 1997), p. 13.

'Oh, To Be Clean', *Ruach* (October/November 1997), p. 17.

'Three Pictures' and 'Then There Were None', *Ruach* (January 1998), p. 21.

'Slave Labourers Still Living in Dire Poverty', *The Holocaust Survivors' Centre News* (March 1996), p. 17.

Book review of *Who was David Weiser?* by Pawel Huelle [transl. from Polish by Antonina Lloyd], *The Holocaust Survivors' Centre News* (March 1996), p. 17.

'Speaking About the Holocaust in Various Countries: The Personal Experiences of Trude Levi', *The Holocaust Survivors' Centre News* (September 1996), p. 8.

'Why Oh Why: or Race Prejudice', *The Holocaust Survivors' Centre News*, 6 (Spring 1998), p. 30.

'Films on the Holocaust as an Educational Resource', *The Holocaust Survivors' Centre News*, 7 (Spring 2000) p. 17.

'Speaking Out: The Education Work of a Holocaust Survivor', *The Journal of Holocaust Education, Museums and the Holocaust* (Winter 1998), pp. 113–22, originally written for a lecture at Sussex University, December 1998.

'All My Friends: The Story of Three Pictures', *Perspective* (Winter 1998), p. 16.
'Some Thoughts about My Role in Holocaust Teaching', *Our Congregation*, 513 (September 1999), p. 4.
Book review of *Making Memory: Creating Britain's First Holocaust Centre* by Stephen Smith, *Congregation*, 520 (May 2000), p. 5.
'Erinnerungen an Franz Levi (1920–1999)', *Historische Kommission für Thüringen e.V. Kleine Vortragsreihe. Heft 3. Franz Levi und Berkach. Ansprachen und Vorträge bei der Präsentation des Buches: 12 Gulden vom Judengeld … Jüdisches Leben in Berkach und Südwestthüringen.* Compiled and annotated by Franz Levi, with collaboration of Johannes Mötsch, Katharina Witter (Historische Kommission für Thüringen, Grosse Reihe, Bd.7 am 6. Mai 2001 in der Synagogue in Berkach), pp. 20–4.

## Suggested Further Reading

Bauer, Yehuda, 'The Death Marches, January–May 1945', *Modern Judaism* 3 (1983), pp. 1–21.
Braham, Randolph L., *The Politics of Genocide: Holocaust in Hungary* (New York: Columbia University Press, 1980).
Browning, Christopher, *Ordinary Men, Reserve Police Bataliion 101 and the Final Solution in Poland* (New York: Harper-Collins, 1992).
Espelage, Gregor, *'Friedland' bei Hessisch-Lichtenau. Geschichte einer Stadt und Sprengstoffabrik in der Zeit des Dritten Reiches in zwei Bänden*, Vol. 2, *Geschichte der Sprengstoffabrik Hessisch-Lichtenau* (Hessisch-Lichtenau [Hrsg: Stadt Hessisch-Lichtenau, 1994).
Facing History and Ourselves, *Holocaust and Human Behavior* (Brookline, MA: Facing History and Ourselves National Foundation, Inc., 1994).
Gilbert, Martin, *The Holocaust* (London: Fontana, 1987).
Goldhagen, Daniel, *Hitler's Willing Executioners: Ordinary Germans and the Holocaust* (New York: Knopf, 1996).
Hilberg, Raul, *The Destruction of the European Jews*, 3 Vols. rev. edn (New York: Holmes & Meier, 1985).
Holliday, Laurel (ed.), *Children's Wartime Diaries: Secret Writings from the Holocaust and World War II* (London: Piatkus, 1995).
Isaacson, Judith Magyar, *Seeds of Sarah: Memoirs of a Survivor* (Chicago, IL: University of Illinois Press, 1990).
Koenig, Wolfram and Schneider, Ulrich, *Vergangenheit und Gegenwart einer Munitionsfabrik*, in Gesamthochschule Kassel (ed.), vol. 8, *National-sozialismus in Nordhessen: Schriftenreihe zur regionaler Zeitgeschichte* (Kassel, 1984).

Lipstadt, Deborah E., *Denying the Holocaust: The Growing Assault on Truth and Memory* (London: Penguin Books Ltd, 1993).

Marrus, Michael R., *The Unwanted: European Refugees in the Twentieth Century* (Boston, MA: Oxford University Press Inc., 1985).

Nissim, Luciana, *Ricordi della case dei morti, Donne contro il mostro* (Turin: Vicenzo Ramella, 1946).

Rothkirchen, Livia, 'The "Final Solution" in the Last Stages', *Yad Vashem Studies*, 8 (1970), pp. 7–28.

*The Journal of Holocaust Education* (London: Frank Cass, 1992) [journal].

Vaupel, Dieter, *Spuren die nicht vergehen [Traces which do not disappear]: Eine Studie über Zwangsarbeit und Entschädigung*, 2nd edn (Kassel: Verlag Gesamthochschul-Bibliothek, 2001).

Vincent, Victoria Ancona, *Beyond Imagination, Witness Collection* (Laxton: Beth Shalom Ltd, 1995).

# Index

# Book of Related Interest

# A Cat Called Adolf
## Trude Levi

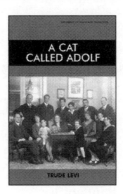

*"...young adults should read it as a corrective to the common misconceptions of today, its inner message is one for all generations and seasons...as a drop in the ocean of world history it has something to tell us all"*

**The Junior Bookshelf**

*"The reader cannot help but marvel at her resilience and adaptability"*

**The Jewish Chronicle**

This is one Holocaust memoir which does not stop at survival but goes on to describe the lasting effects of the persecution, betrayal and suffering upon those survivors.

Forty years after the Holocaust, on holiday in Germany, Trude Levi came across a cat named Adolf, so called because it used to raise its paw. It revived many bitter memories of her experiences as a young Hungarian girl deported to Auschwitz, and made her realise the importance of telling the story – and the lessons – of her survival.

Her most fervent wish in telling her story is that the lessons of the Holocaust are never forgotten, and that the events she recorded are never allowed to happen again.

**176 pages illus 1994 3rd reprint 2002**
**0 85303 289 0 paper £11.95/$17.45**

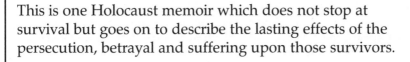

**VALLENTINE MITCHELL**
Crown House, 47 Chase Side, Southgate, London N14 5BP
Tel: +44 (0)20 8920 2100  Fax: +44 (0)20 8447 8548  E-mail: info@vmbooks.com
**NORTH AMERICA**
5824 NE Hassalo Street, Portland, OR 97213-3644, USA
Tel: 800 944 6190  Fax: 503 280 8832  E-mail: orders@isbs.com
**Website:** www.vmbooks.com

# Journal of Related Interest

# The Journal of Holocaust Education

Editors **Dr Jo Reilly**, *University of Southampton* and
**Dr Donald Bloxham**, *University of Edinburgh*

*The Journal of Holocaust Education*, now celebrating its 10th anniversary, has established itself as an important resource for teachers, both inside and outside the university sector, and as a forum for debate for all those interested in Holocaust education. It is devoted to all aspects of interdisciplinary Holocaust education and research, and reaches a wide audience including scholars in Britain and overseas, students, and the general reader interested in both the Jewish and the non-Jewish experience. Apart from authoritative and informed articles (including examples of outstanding student work) *The Journal of Holocaust Education* carries: conference and workshop reports; book, video and film reviews; useful information on where to find primary source materials; and bulletins on forthcoming events.

**Forthcoming Articles**
**Holocaust Curricula in Israeli Secondary Schools, 1960–1990s** by *Yuval Dror*
**The Memory of Forced Labour in Nuremburg** by *Neil Gregor*
**Holocaust Education for the New Millennium**
by *Mary J. Gallant and Harriet Hartman*

ISSN 1359-1371  Volume 11 2003
Three issues per year
Individuals £32/$45  Institutions £95/$145
New individual introductory subscriber rate £25/$36

**VALLENTINE MITCHELL**
Crown House, 47 Chase Side, Southgate, London N14 5BP
Tel: +44 (0)20 8920 2100  Fax: +44 (0)20 8447 8548  E-mail: info@vmbooks.com
**NORTH AMERICA**
5824 NE Hassalo Street, Portland, OR 97213-3644, USA
Tel: 800 944 6190  Fax: 503 280 8832  E-mail: orders@isbs.com
**Website:** www.vmbooks.com

# Library of Holocaust Testimonies

**Warsaw Ghetto Thermopolye**
Leslaw Bartelski

**Journey through Darkness:
Monowitz, Auschwitz,
Gross-Rosen, Buchenwald**
Willy Berler

**Like Leaves in the Wind**
Rita Blumstein

**Six From Leipzig**
Gertrude Dubrovsky

**Fortuna's Children**
Paul and Eric Fahidi

**From the Edge of the World**
Anne Joseph

**Back to the Old Country**
Dovid Katz

**A Jewish Life: A Memoir**
Zev Katz

**Fire without Smoke: The
Memoirs of a Polish Partisan**
Florian Mayevski *with* Spencer
Bright

**Jazz Survivor: The Story of
Louis Bannet, Horn Player of
Auschwitz**
Ken Shuldman

**Socially Unreliable: Surviving
the Holocaust in Stalin's Russia**
Henrik Skorr *with* Ivan Sokolov

**Hasag-Leipzig Slave Labour
Camp for Women**
Dr Felicja Karay

**Good Beyond Evil**
Eva Gossman

**By a Twist of History**
Mietek Sieradzi

**Scenes from the Warsaw Ghetto**
Luca Kresy

**To Forgive…But not Forget:
Maja's Story**
Maja Abramowitch

**A Little House on Mount
Carmel**
Alexandre Blumstein

**Aspects of Fear**
Henryk Vogler

**For Love of Life**
Leah Iglinski-Goodman

**The Jews of Poznan**
Zbigniew Pakula

**From Berlin to England and
Back: Experiences of a Jewish
Berliner**
Peter Prager

**VALLENTINE MITCHELL**
Crown House, 47 Chase Side, Southgate, London N14 5BP
Tel: +44 (0)20 8920 2100  Fax: +44 (0)20 8447 8548  E-mail: info@vmbooks.com
**NORTH AMERICA**
5824 NE Hassalo Street, Portland, OR 97213-3644, USA
Tel: 800 944 6190  Fax: 503 280 8832  E-mail: orders@isbs.com
**Website:** www.vmbooks.com

# Library of Holocaust Testimonies

**No Place to Run**
David Gilbert
*Written by* Tim Shortridge and
Michael D. Frountfelter

**An Englishman in Auschwitz**
Leon Greenman

**Who are You, Mr Grymek?**
Natan Gross

**From Thessaloniki to Auschwitz
and Back 1926–1996**
Erika Myriam Kounio Amariglio

**A Life Sentence of Memories**
Issy Hahn

**Out of the Ghetto**
Jack Klajman *with* Ed Klajman

**Surviving the Nazis, Exhile and
Siberia**
Edith Sekules

**My Child is Back!**
Ursula Pawel

**I was No. 20832 at Auschwitz**
Eva Tichauer

**Wartime Experiences in
Lithuania**
Rivka Lozansky Bogomolnaya
*Edited by* Susan Logan
*Translated by* Miriam Beckerman

**Have You Seen My Little Sister?**
Janina Fischler-Martinho

**Memoirs from Occupied
Warsaw 1940–1945**
Helena Szerszewska
*Translated by* Anna Marinska

**My Heart in a Suitcase**
Anne L. Fox

**The Children Accuse**
Maria Hochberg-Maianska and
Noe Gruss

**A Child Alone**
Martha Blend

**I Light A Candle**
Gene Turgel *with* Veronica
Groocock

**A Cat Called Adolf**
Trude Levi

**An End to Childhood**
Miriam Akavia

**My Lost World**
Sara Rosen

**My Private War**
Jacob Gerstenfeld-Maltiel

**From Dachau to Dunkirk**
Fred Pelican

**VALLENTINE MITCHELL**
Crown House, 47 Chase Side, Southgate, London N14 5BP
Tel: +44 (0)20 8920 2100  Fax: +44 (0)20 8447 8548  E-mail: info@vmbooks.com
**NORTH AMERICA**
5824 NE Hassalo Street, Portland, OR 97213-3644, USA
Tel: 800 944 6190  Fax: 503 280 8832  E-mail: orders@isbs.com
**Website:** www.vmbooks.com